BEAN COOKERY

Sue & Bill Deeming

ANOTHER BEST-SELLING COOKERY VOLUME FROM H.P. BOOKS

Publisher: Helen Fisher; Editor: Carlene Tejada; Art Director: Don Burton; Book Design: Kathy Olson; Typography: Cindy Coatsworth, Joanne Porter; Food Stylist: Janet Pittman; Photography: George deGennaro Studios.

The authors wish to thank the following for their contributions to this book: Dorothy Deeming and William S. Deeming; Ed Fash, Westlam Foods, Inc.; Gordon Monfort, California Dry Bean Advisory Board; L. B. Rockland, U.S. Department of Agriculture; Bill Prusse, Beans of the West; Mr. Rogers and staff, Gallant Carroll Hardware, Tucson.

NOTICE: The information contained in this book is true and complete to the best of our knowledge. All recommendations are made without any guarantees on the part of the authors or HPBooks. The authors and publisher disclaim all liability incurred in connection with the use of this information.

Published by H.P. Books, P.O. Box 5367, Tucson, AZ 85703   602/888-2150
ISBN 0-89586-037-6
Library of Congress Catalog Card Number 79-92582 © 1980 Fisher Publishing, Inc.
Printed in U.S.A.

Cover Photo: Southern-Style Baked Beans, page 84

What Are Beans?

Beans, lentils and peas are classified as *legumes:* plants with seed-filled pods. These seeds and pods are what you know as the different varieties of beans, peas and lentils. The various legumes have much in common, including the ability of their seeds to be dried and stored for long periods.

Legumes can be eaten at different stages in their life cycles. Bean sprouts are the roots of bean seeds. Green beans, also called *string beans* and *snap beans*, are the tender immature pods enclosing the bean seeds. Mature bean pods are tough and inedible, but the seeds or dried beans and peas, are plump and delicious

Dried beans, lentils and peas can be used in soups, cooked as a vegetable or combined with other protein foods to make a main dish. To add even more variety, cooked dried legumes can be mixed, mashed, molded, pureed or prepared in a number of other ways to create an array of foods from peasant-style stews and casseroles to gourmet salads and intriguing desserts.

Bean Cookery concentrates on 25 of the edible seeds or beans in the legume category. Of these 25 varieties, 17 are grown commercially in the United States and packaged as dried beans. Many are also available in stores as canned cooked dried beans. Canellini beans and dark red kidney beans are only available canned. Green beans, wax beans, Italian beans, baby lima beans, green peas and snow peas are available canned and fresh or frozen.

DRIED BEANS & NEW RESEARCH

Dried beans are unique in the food world. They are a raw agricultural product and one of the few foods still on grocery store shelves requiring both processing and cooking in the home. Until recently, very little research had been done with dried beans and methods for cooking them. With what we know today, cooking dried beans does not require the commitments of time or attention that you may think. New agricultural techniques, modern transportation and storage methods, and advances in cooking procedures have reduced the attention and time needed to cook beans.

Although cooking dried beans cannot be completely standardized, enough knowledge is available to dismiss many common beliefs as folklore or superstitions.

The recipes in this book have been created and tested to ensure your success in bean and legume cookery.

NUTRITION

A meal of properly cooked dried beans, lentils or peas provides significant amounts of protein, minerals, vitamins and fiber. Most fresh legumes that are eaten before their seeds reach maturity are not as high in nutritive value as dried mature seeds. Examples are green beans and green peas.

PROTEIN

Protein contributes to the growth of new body cells and maintains the constant process of replacing worn cells with new ones. Proteins are made up of amino acids. There are two kinds of proteins.

Complete proteins are animal proteins found in meat, fish, poultry, eggs and dairy products. They contain all necessary amino acids to fulfill protein requirements.

Incomplete proteins are plant proteins found in fruits, vegetables, nuts, grains and other legumes. Because they all lack some amino acids they are classified as incomplete proteins.

Complementing proteins is a method for improving the nutritive quality of incomplete proteins. There are two ways to do this.

The easiest and most reliable method is to serve a small amount of a complete protein with the incomplete protein. You can sprinkle an ounce or two of shredded cheese on the beans, or add a small piece of chicken or sausage to the plate. Most recipes in this book include a small amount of complete protein to increase the value of the bean protein.

A second method of complementing proteins is to combine incomplete protein foods with each other, choosing those that make up for the other's weaknesses. With beans, you would serve rice, corn, or wheat. The combined amino acids of these incomplete proteins supply a more complete protein than either one does alone. Complementary proteins may be cooked together in the same dish or served separately at the same meal.

MINERALS

Cooked, dried beans are a rich source of iron, the nutrient most often lacking in today's diets. A cup of most varieties of cooked, dried beans supplies almost half of a man's daily iron need or about one-fourth of a woman's need.

Beans also supply phosphorus, magnesium, calcium, potassium and other minerals. These minerals are important nutrients, although not much is yet known about how well they are utilized from beans.

VITAMINS

Cooked, dried beans are among the richest sources of several B-complex vitamins, including thiamine (B_1), pyriodoxine (B_6) and folic acid. Beans also supply important amounts of riboflavin (B_2) and niacin.

OTHER NUTRITIONAL FACTORS

Beans contain a high proportion of carbohydrates which accounts for the full feeling you have after eating a bean meal. Luckily, this full feeling comes with only 250 or less calories per cup of beans, depending upon the type of bean. In addition, beans have very little fat—only what you add in cooking. Beans contain no cholesterol unless animal fats are added for flavor.

Beans are a great source of fiber or bulk necessary for normal digestion and elimination. Although information is incomplete, fiber may be a very important health factor for people who eat large quantities of highly refined and processed foods.

Sue & Bill Deeming

Cooking supper together is one way to start a cookbook. But in 1969, right after their marriage, the idea of a cookbook hadn't occurred to either of the Deemings. Bill was soon trying to recreate the hearty bean dishes of his Southwestern heritage. The next step was *Bean Cookery*.

Sue's background includes a Masters Degree in Home Economics and Nutrition and a Ph.D. in Agricultural Biochemistry and Nutrition. She has designed and managed a retail market, worked on new product development for a well-known food corporation, and planned and supervised kitchen operations for a large restaurant. She has taught courses in nutrition, meal planning and international cuisines. She is currently a food and nutrition consultant.

Bill has a B.A. degree from the University of Arizona in Communications and Psychology and a Masters Degree from San Francisco Theological Seminary. He has been active in family and individual counseling through pastoral and community counseling services.

Sue and Bill were helped in preparing and sampling bean recipes by their daughter, Eryn.

How To Buy Dried Beans

When you buy dried beans, inspect the package. Most of the beans should be whole and have firm, unbroken seed coats. Less than 10 percent should be broken, wrinkled and blistered. Beans should also be uniform in size and color with few rust spots or discolorations. Not more than 1 percent of the beans should show insect damage marked by holes and cavities.

Large lima beans are more susceptible to being broken or having broken seed coats than are the other bean varieties. While these broken, wrinkled or blistered beans may affect the appearance of the finished bean dish, the taste and nutritional quality of the beans will still be excellent.

CAN'T FIND THE BEAN YOU WANT?

All the dried beans used in this book are or can be available to all consumers. If you can't find the bean you want, it is because there is no demand in that store for that bean. If you add your request to those already received by the store manager, you may soon find the store carrying that particular bean. Store managers don't know what you need if you don't tell them.

How To Store Dried Beans

Dried beans can be stored a relatively long period of time, but not forever! With correct storage, their quality can be maintained 6 months to 1 year. If kept too long, they will lose too much moisture and will not rehydrate or cook satisfactorily. If stored incorrectly, the beans may absorb water and spoil before you have a chance to use them.

The plastic bags beans are packaged in are good for storage if they are airtight. Once opened, the bag may be reclosed with a twist tie. For the longest storage life, keep beans in a glass or plastic container with a tight-fitting lid. Store them in a cool dry place.

Canned Beans

Almost all varieties of dried beans are commercially cooked and canned, although they all may not be available in every area. Some beans, such as dark red kidney beans and white kidney or cannellini beans, are only available canned. Garbanzo beans and wax beans are usually bought canned. Dried garbanzo beans can also be purchased packaged or in bulk. Wax beans can sometimes be found fresh during the summer months.

How To Prepare Dried Beans

Dried beans go through a series of thrashing and sifting processes to remove pods, foreign material and undersized beans before packaging. This mechanical processing does not remove all the small stones, soil clods and dust. You must continue the process by sorting and rinsing the beans at home.

SORTING

Sorting means picking over the beans before cooking them. Remove small rocks, pieces of dirt, beans with holes or cavities, badly misshapen or wrinkled beans and those greatly undersized or discolored.

When sorting beans, remove those that have holes, are broken, discolored or very small. Remove any other varieties of beans and any foreign matter such as dirt or small stones.

RINSING

Washing is not part of the packing process because water would rehydrate the beans. Do not rinse beans until you are ready to soak or cook them. Even then, you do not have to rinse beans if you're going to soak them. Any field dust will be removed by soaking and discarded with the soak water.

If you cook beans without soaking, rinse them after sorting. Legumes that don't require soaking, such as black-eyed peas, lentils and split peas, should be rinsed before cooking.

SOAKING

Soaking is not an essential step in bean preparation. The purpose of soaking is to begin rehydration before cooking, thereby reducing cooking time. Unsoaked beans take longer to cook and require more attention so they won't cook dry.

During soaking, beans take up their lost water, increasing up to twice their dried size. Enough water must be used to keep the beans covered while soaking. Once rehydrated, beans cook in 1 to 3 hours, depending on the type of bean.

There are two methods for soaking: long-soak and quick-soak. Both work equally well and differ only in the amount of time required to rehydrate the beans. Choose the one which best suits your time and schedule.

Long-soaking takes time and some advance planning, but needs very little effort. First, cover the beans with water at room temperature. Soak them overnight or for 8 to 10 hours. Keep the beans covered by water while soaking. Be sure the soak water is at room temperature. Hot water may cause the beans to sour. Cold water slows rehydration and the beans will take longer to cook. Cooking time will also be longer if beans are not soaked long enough—at least 8 hours. Beans soaked longer than 12 hours can absorb too much water and lose their characteristic texture and flavor.

If you plan to cook beans for dinner and you want to use the long-soak method, start soaking in the morning. To cook beans for lunch, you'll have to soak them overnight.

Quick-soaking rehydrates dried beans in little more than 1 hour. For most cooks, this is the most convenient method. Bring the beans and water for soaking to a boil. Boil for 2 minutes. Remove the beans from the heat and cover the pot. Let the beans stand in the soak water for 1 hour. At the end of the hour, discard the soak water and cook the beans. Don't let them stand in hot soak water longer than 2 to 3 hours or they may spoil.

COOKING WITHOUT SOAKING

Beans don't have to be soaked before they are cooked. Soaking merely shortens cooking time. Because unsoaked beans have to cook longer, they require more energy from your stove.

To cook beans without soaking, use twice the amount of cooking water specified in the recipe. Combine the water and rinsed beans in the pot and bring to a boil. Some cooks like to bring the water to a boil first, then drop in the beans a few at a time so the boiling doesn't stop. Either method will cook the beans satisfactorily. Cover the pot and reduce the heat to maintain a simmer. The beans rehydrate while cooking so you will have to watch them carefully and add more water whenever necessary to keep them covered.

Cooking time for unsoaked beans can vary up to 2 hours. Most beans will be tender in 2 to 3 hours. Don't go by the cooking times given on page 15 or in the recipes throughout the book. These times apply only to soaked beans.

Dried beans more than double their volume in the cooking process. The dried beans in the measuring cup at the bottom of the photo have not been cooked or soaked.

How To Cook Dried Beans

Dried beans can be cooked in a saucepan or pot on top of the stove, in a pressure cooker, or in your oven.

The basic principles of cooking dried beans remain the same no matter which method you use. Dried beans require water or other liquid, oil or other fat and salt. Any acidic ingredients called for must be added at the specified time.

Water or other liquid is needed to soften the beans as they cook. There must be enough liquid to keep the beans covered so they will cook uniformly. Any beans not covered during cooking will dry out and be inedible.

Oil or other fat is used in the cooking of many foods to lessen the possibility of the cooking water boiling over. Vegetable oil, butter or margarine, lard or bacon is usually added to beans to help prevent boilovers. The oil or fat used in the cooking also adds flavor to the beans.

Salt is necessary to give beans flavor. There is some controversy as to when is the best time to add the salt to the beans. Some cooks add the salt only after the beans have been softened in cooking. Others prefer to add the salt to the cooking water with the beans. Our experience is that adding salt at the beginning of cooking results in more flavorful beans and does not significantly influence the cooking time or tenderness of the beans.

Acidic Ingredients such as tomatoes, vinegar, ketchup, chili sauce or lemon juice retard the cooking and softening of beans. Recipes in this book specify when to add these acidic ingredients so they will not delay the cooking process.

STOVE-TOP COOKING

Cooking beans on top of the stove is a slow process that allows the flavors of the beans and seasoning to intermingle, creating the hearty flavor you expect from bean dishes. The disadvantage of this method is that it requires you to be present, although not continuously involved, while the beans are cooking.

To cook beans on your stove-top, combine soaked or dried beans, water, oil or fat, and seasonings in a saucepan or pot of appropriate size. Bring the beans to a boil, reduce the heat, then cover and simmer until the beans are tender. This takes 30 minutes to 3 hours, depending on the bean variety. Check the beans occasionally to see if they are covered with the cooking liquid. If there is so much liquid absorption and evaporation that the top of the beans becomes exposed, add very hot tap water to the pot to cover the beans.

When dried beans boil, a foam forms on the top of the cooking liquid. This foam is water-soluble protein released from the beans and it will be absorbed back into the bean cooking liquid. It is not necessary to remove the foam.

The best cookware for beans is a heavy metal pot or saucepan. Stainless steel, cast aluminum or cast iron are all excellent. The following guide may help you decide which of your pots and pans would be best for cooking beans.

Stainless-steel pans should have copper or aluminum bottoms to distribute heat evenly. This cookware is easy to care for and lasts a lifetime.

Cast-aluminum pans must be heavy to distribute heat well. Aluminum darkens with use but this does not affect the quality of the cookware or the cooked beans. Thin aluminum pans are inappropriate for cooking beans.

Cast iron is the heaviest of stove-top cookware. It heats slowly, distributes heat evenly and holds heat better than other materials. Cast iron coated with porcelain enamel is easy to clean.

A saucepan or pot must have a tight-fitting lid. The lid should have a lip that fits closely around the inside of the saucepan or pot to prevent steam from escaping as the beans simmer. When evaporation losses are minimal, the pot requires less watching.

PRESSURE COOKERS

If you have a pressure cooker, take advantage of it to prepare beans in a matter of minutes.

Pressure cookers are specially designed cookware of aluminum or stainless steel. All models have a lock-on lid and a vent over which a weight or pressure regulator is placed. Most pressure cookers are designed to be used on top of your stove, but at least one model has its own electrical heat source.

Food is cooked by the high temperatures inside the cooker. This high temperature is made possible by raising the pressure to a point greater than atmospheric pressure. Fifteen pounds of pressure will raise the temperature in the cooker high enough to cook soaked beans in 3 to 8 minutes. Cooking times given on page 15 are based on 15 pounds of pressure. Some older models cook at 10 pounds pressure. If your cooker uses only 10 pounds, double the cooking time.

Before cooking beans in your pressure cooker, read the manufacturer's instructions.

Safety Measures—All pressure cookers have built-in safety mechanisms:

• An *over-pressure plug* prevents pressure in the cooker from increasing if the regulator vent becomes clogged. To make sure this vent is clear, hold the lid up to the light and look through the vent. If the vent is closed or evenly partially closed, unplug it before using the cooker.

• A lock-on-lid prevents the cooker from being opened if there is still pressure inside.

Cooking Beans In Your Pressure Cooker—Combine soaked beans, water or other cooking liquid, vegetable oil and seasonings in the cooker. Do not fill it more than half full. Following the manufacturer's instructions, seal the cooker and bring it up to the required pressure.

When the pressure regulator indicates the proper pressure, reduce the heat and start timing. Maintain heat under the cooker so the regulator moves gently or rocks 1 to 3 times per minute, as indicated for your type of cooker. If the regulator does not move at all, pressure is not being maintained because the heat is too low. If the regulator is in constant motion, the heat is too high. Cook for the shortest specified time indicated in Bean Cooking Times, page 15.

Remove the cooker from the heat. To prevent beans from overcooking, follow the manufacturer's instructions for quickly reducing the pressure in your cooker. To be sure the pressure has completely dropped, jiggle the regulator. If there in no hiss of steam, there is no longer any pressure.

Remove the regulator and lid and taste a few beans. If they are not as tender as you like, finish cooking without pressure. To do this, bring the beans to a boil over medium heat. Reduce the heat to maintain the beans at a simmer. Place the lid on the cooker but **do not lock it. And do not use the weight, or pressure regulator.** Simmer for 15 to 30 minutes until the beans are tender.

If you have to cook beans longer on top of the stove after they have cooked in the pressure cooker, add 1 minute to the pressure-cooking time the next time you cook them. Continue to add a minute every time you cook beans until they are done to the tenderness you like.

High altitude (above 3,500 feet) will at least double the time needed for cooking beans under pressure, see page 9. Check the manufacturer's instructions if you live in a high-altitude area.

Because the cooking time in a pressure cooker is so short, the beans may not absorb the flavor from the seasonings as well as when they cook in a saucepan or pot. Some cooks let the beans stand 30 minutes or so after cooking in the pressure cooker to help them absorb the flavorings. Other cooks prefer to use the stove-top method when they want a highly flavored bean dish.

Pressure Cooker Tips

• Before cooking beans in your pressure cooker, remove the rack, or trivet, from inside the cooker.

• Do not fill your pressure cooker more than half full of beans and water or cooking liquid.

• When you close your cooker, be sure the lid is closed tightly and locked. If the lid is not closed and locked, steam will escape and the necessary pressure for cooking will not build up.

• **Never remove the weight, or pressure regulator, while pressure is still in the cooker.** This releases steam which is dangerously hot! To see if any pressure remains in the cooker, jiggle the weight on the vent. If you can see or hear steam escaping, you know there is still pressure in the cooker.

OVEN COOKING

Baking in the hot dry air of the oven is a slow process, but it's the only way to create the glazed, crusty top characteristic of baked beans and bean pot casseroles. Generally, oven cooking is used in combination with cooking in a pressure cooker or in a saucepan on top of the stove. Be sure the beans are not overcooked before baking or they will be mushy.

Traditional containers for baking beans are earthenware bean pots, usually 3- or 3-1/2-quart size. The pot and lid should be glazed at least on the inside and must be lead-free. You can also use glass or ceramic casseroles. Metal baking pans are not recommended.

To bake beans, preheat the oven according to the recipe instructions. Then combine the drained cooked beans, seasonings, liquids and any other ingredients in the bean pot or casserole. Cover it and bake for 1 to 1-1/2 hours. To brown the top of the beans, remove the lid and bake the beans 15 to 30 minutes longer. Bean pot recipes start on page 74.

CROCK POTS (ELECTRIC SLOW COOKERS)

The advantage of using a crock pot is that you can put the food in it, turn it on and forget it. Several hours later, the dish is ready to eat. But beans do not cook that simply in a crock pot. The Low setting is too low, lengthening the cooking time to 16 or 20 hours. And depending upon the age of the beans and the hardness of the water, the beans may not cook at all! If you cook beans on the High setting, a large amount of cooking liquid evaporates. You'll have to watch the crock pot to be sure the beans stay covered with liquid.

If you want to experiment with your crock pot, try cooking soaked beans for 2 or 3 hours on High, making sure they are constantly covered by liquid. When they are just tender, turn the heat setting to Low and let them cook 6 to 8 hours longer. During these last 6 to 8 hours the beans won't need any special attention.

Crock pots can be used to reheat pre-cooked beans. They are also useful for keeping bean soups and stews warm while you finish preparing a meal or for serving at a buffet.

UNTIL TENDER

Recipes in this book tell you to cook beans *until*

High Altitudes

As altitude increases, dried beans take more time to rehydrate and cook. The difference begins to be noticeable above 3,500 feet.

Your pressure cooker can be useful at high altitudes but you'll have to experiment with the cooking time. Begin by doubling the pressure cooker time in Bean Cooking Times, page 15. Finish cooking on top of the stove as directed.

Information on high-altitude cooking is available from your Cooperative Extension Service.

---

tender. To check for tenderness, pinch or bite a few beans at the minimum suggested time, then every 10 to 15 minutes until the beans are tender.

Overcooked beans fall apart, releasing bean starch which thickens the cooking liquid. This may be desirable for some recipes.

LEFTOVERS

Leftover beans should be cooled and then refrigerated in an airtight container. They will usually keep at least 4 days.

Bean dishes thicken as they cool and their seasonings and flavors continue to blend. That's why bean dishes are better the next day.

Reheat beans over low heat and stir them often. Beans scorch easily over high heat. If the beans are too thick, stir in some water a little at a time.

Preparing more beans than you need is the best way to get valuable leftovers. With leftover beans and the recipes in this book, you can make quick, easy lunches, salads or appetizers.

FREEZING COOKED BEANS

Any of the Basic Beans, pages 14 to 19, freeze well. If you plan to freeze all of the beans you cook, it's a good idea to undercook them. This usually means cooking about 30 minutes less than the suggested cooking times. If you cook beans in your pressure cooker, reduce the cooking time by 1 to 1-1/2 minutes. Undercooking will help the beans maintain their shape and texture as they thaw and reheat.

Freeze beans in 1- to 2-cup portions so they'll be easy to thaw and use. Freezer containers should be airtight and moisture-proof. Leave enough space at the top of the container for expansion of the beans. Fill the container to 1 to 1 1/2 inches from the top, making sure the beans are covered with liquid so they won't dry out.

Cooked beans will keep in the freezer 2 to 3 months. After that time their flavor and texture will begin to deteriorate.

THAWING & REHEATING FROZEN BEANS

Beans maintain their shape better if they are thawed slowly. Thaw them overnight in the refrigerator, for several hours at room temperature, or for about an hour in a pan of warm water. When the beans can be removed from their freezer container, put them in a saucepan to reheat and finish cooking.

Bring the beans to a boil slowly over medium heat to avoid scorching. Then reduce the heat and simmer until the beans are tender, 20 to 30 minutes. The time the beans need to simmer will depend on how undercooked they were when you froze them. If they were fully cooked before freezing, you need only reheat them.

MICROWAVE OVENS

Microwave ovens are not satisfactory for cooking dried legumes because long slow simmering is required for complete rehydration and cooking. A microwave is a time-saver for thawing or reheating.

Thaw frozen beans in their plastic or glass freezer container. Remove the lid and cover beans loosely with plastic wrap or waxed paper. Microwave on **Defrost** or the setting recommended by the manufacturer for thawing. Thawing time varies with the amount of beans and the setting used. Do not thaw completely; beans should be icy in the center. Let them stand covered at room temperature 2 to 3 minutes to finish thawing.

If beans were undercooked when frozen, finish cooking them in a saucepan on top of the stove.

To reheat beans, cover with a glass lid, plastic wrap or waxed paper. Beans will pop when reheated on **High** so use **Medium** or the setting recommended by the manufacturer. Heating time varies with the amount of beans. Stir them at least once while reheating; let them stand 5 minutes to distribute the heat evenly.

Using a microwave oven to finish casseroles or main dishes may save up to an hour. Assemble the casserole. Cover and cook on a medium setting. Use the cooking time of a similar microwave recipe as a guide. Let the casserole stand 5 minutes before serving.

Common Dried Beans

Many dried bean varieties are known by different names according to where you live. This creates a great deal of confusion—especially with recipes. These pictures of the beans, their common package names and other names they go by should help you chose the right bean for the recipe you are following.

Mung Beans make beautiful, crisp, tasty bean sprouts. They are frequently used in oriental cooking but are growing in popularity for general use. Health-food stores and Oriental-food stores carry dried mung beans. Some supermarkets carry canned bean sprouts and frequently stock fresh ones. For how to sprout mung beans, see Sprouts, pages 12 and 13.

Lentils are widely available dried and are probably used in more areas of the world than any other legume. They are used in such wholesome dishes as Lentil Soup & Dumplings, page 48. Lentils can also be sprouted. See pages 12 and 13 for sprouting directions.

Green Split Peas are widely available dried. They can be substituted for Yellow Split Peas. Ham and split peas go well together. And they combine best in Old-Fashioned Split Pea Soup, page 46.

Yellow Split Peas are available but are sometimes more difficult to find than green split peas. When you do find them, try Split Pea Soup With Mushrooms, page 46.

Black Beans, *turtle beans* or *black turtle beans* are only packaged dried but are not in all supermarkets. You might find them in stores that carry Spanish or Oriental foods. Black beans are popular throughout Latin America and are a necessary ingredient for Brazilian Bean Soup, page 43.

Soybeans are usually available in health-food stores and sometimes can be found in supermarkets. They can be bought dried and may sometimes be canned. High in nutritional content, their use is steadily increasing. Soybeans can be served in a variety of ways. Try Soybean Spread, page 26.

Black-Eyed Peas are also known as *black-eyed beans* and *cowpeas*. Look for them dried, canned and frozen. They are a staple in the southern United States. For a typical dish of that area, try Hoppin' John, page 115.

Garbanzo Beans, which you may know as *chick peas* or *ceci beans,* are more common canned than dried. Their flavor is somewhat nutty. Garbanzos are enjoyed in many countries, including Spain and Italy. They are best known in Hummus, page 135, an appetizer from the Middle East.

Red Beans, also known as *red Mexican beans, small red beans, California red beans* and *Idaho red beans,* may be difficult to find, depending on where you live. Look for them both canned and dried. You can use red kidney beans as a substitute. Red beans are an interesting addition to Salami & Rice Salad, page 57.

Pink Beans may be available regionally from time to time. If the stores in your area don't carry them, substitute pinto beans. So far the bean industry does not can pink beans. Pink beans are good as a side dish in Western Beans, page 17.

Pinto Beans are the staple for Mexican cooking, but they are widely available dried and canned. They are extremely versatile. Pureed pinto beans are needed to make Apple Surprise Cake, page 154. Bean Puree, page 18, is also used in other recipes.

Red Kidney beans may be labeled *Light Red Kidney Beans.* Look for them dried or canned. They have almost world-wide popularity and are in demand for such dishes as Mama's Homemade Chili, page 47.

Pea Beans or *navy beans* have regional distribution. If you can't find them in your area, use small white beans. You may be able to buy cooked dried pea or navy beans in cans in your area. Pea beans are used to make baked beans, or bean pots such as Boston Baked Beans, page 83.

Great Northern Beans or *Great Northerns* are commonly found dried. They have a delicate flavor which makes them a good choice for salads such as Sunshine Salad, page 53. You may find canned Great Northerns. Substitute canned **canellini beans** for canned Great Northerns. Canellini beans are also called *white kidney beans.* They are not available dried.

Small White Beans have no companion large white bean. They are much like pea beans and may be substituted for them. However, you'll only be able to buy small white beans dried. For something different, serve them in African Peanut Soup, page 142.

Baby Lima Beans are also called *small lima beans.* Dried baby limas are white; fresh, frozen and canned baby limas are light green. Lima Beans are traditionally combined with corn to make Succotash, page 131.

Large Lima Beans may be more familiar to you as *butter beans.* Like small lima beans, the dried ones are white. Fresh, frozen and canned large limas are light green. Speckled lima beans, called *calico butter beans,* are used in some areas. Lima Beans are more versatile than you may think; see Tangy Lima Bean Appetizer, page 28.

1/Put sorted mung beans or lentils and water in a 1-quart jar. Cover the jar with cheesecloth, secured with a rubber band. Soak overnight. Drain through the cheesecloth. Rinse and drain again. Place jar on its side and cover with a cloth towel, leaving the top uncovered for ventilation.

2/Seeds will begin to germinate, or sprout, after 24 hours. Rinse and drain the sprouts 3 times a day until they are harvested. You do not have to remove the seeds from the jar or sprouter. We put them in this pie plate so you can see what growing sprouts look like.

Sprouts

Bean sprouts usually refer to sprouted mung beans. They can be found fresh or canned in many supermarkets.

Fresh sprouts spoil very quickly, losing their bright white color and crispness. Do not buy sprouts that are brownish or have a slippery film. Sprouts purchased from a supermarket will stay fresh and crisp only a day or two in the refrigerator.

Canned sprouts keep indefinitely until the can is opened, but they lack the crunchiness and flavor of fresh sprouts.

Lentils can be sprouted but the sprouts are not grown commercially. You can sprout lentils using packaged dried lentils from the supermarket or health-food store.

Mung beans for sprouting are available in health-food stores or Oriental-food stores.

Growing Your Own

With a little planning, you can easily have fresh sprouts whenever you want them.

HOMEMADE SPROUTERS

You don't need expensive equipment. Use a large clean quart jar or canning jar with a wide mouth. Cover the mouth of the jar with cheesecloth or nylon mesh, such as a clean stocking, and secure it with a rubber band. This mesh-like cover will make rinsing and draining easier.

COMMERCIAL SPROUTERS

Sprouters can be purchased in health-food stores and some supermarkets. You can also buy screw rings and a selection of wire screens to fit any wide-mouth jar you may have at home.

Amber-colored glass sprouters limit the amount of light and do not have to be covered.

There also are sprouters designed for growing several types of sprouts at the same time.

HOW TO SPROUT MUNG BEANS & LENTILS

Plan Ahead—Start mung beans sprouting 3 to 5 days before you need them so the sprouts will have time to grow. Lentils need only 3 days. If you are using a quart jar, sprout no more than 1/2 cup of beans or lentils. If you are using a commercial sprouter, follow the manufacturer's directions. First, remove all foreign material and broken seeds.

3/Sprouts are ready to harvest or use when mung bean sprouts are 1 to 2 inches long and lentil sprouts are 1/2 to 3/4 inch long.

4/Gently agitate the sprouts in a bowl of cool water. Remove the loose seed coats that float to the top of the water. Thoroughly drain and refrigerate the sprouts as directed.

Begin Sprouting By Soaking—Pour enough water in the jar or sprouter to cover the mung beans or lentils to 3 or 4 times their depth. Let them stand at room temperature 8 hours or overnight.

Keep Them In The Dark—Drain the sprouts thoroughly. Place the jar on its side and cover it with a dry cloth towel to protect the sprouts from light. Too much light may make them bitter. Do not cover the top of the jar or hide it in a closet or cupboard. Growing sprouts need air. Leave the mesh-covered top of the sprouter uncovered for ventilation. The ideal sprouting temperature is 65° to 75°F (20° to 25°C).

Rinse Often—Beginning sprouts need to be rinsed in room temperature water 3 times a day until they are completely sprouted. Drain them thoroughly after each rinsing. During the last 2 days many of the green seed coats of the mung beans will come loose and can be washed away during rinsing. They are not harmful but some people don't like their bitter taste.

Harvest Without Effort—Mung bean sprouts are ready to eat when they are 1 to 2 inches long. To remove the seed coats from mung-bean sprouts

place them in a large bowl of cool water. Remove the seed coats that float to the surface. Shake the sprouts by the handful in the water to loosen more seed coats. It's not necessary to remove every seed coat. Drain the sprouts and pat them dry with paper towels.

Lentil sprouts are ready when they are 1/2 inch to 3/4 inch long. Their seed coats do not need to be removed.

Refrigerate Sprouts In An Airtight Container—They will keep at least 7 days. They also keep well in a damp paper bag in the refrigerator.

How To Use Sprouts

If you want to eat just plain sprouts, stir-fry them in butter or oil for a few minutes, sprinkle with soy sauce and serve them as a crunchy side dish. Mix bean sprouts with lentil sprouts or alfalfa sprouts and other sprouted grains.

Home-grown sprouts are delicious with vegetables and in salads, soups and sandwiches. For starters, try Sprout Slaw, page 56, Polynesian Boats, page 55, and Sprout & Bean Bake, page 132.

Basic Beans

Beans prepared from the recipes in this section are used as the basic ingredient in many recipes. But keep in mind that beans made from these recipes are delicious by themselves and can be served with any meal.

Most of these Basic Beans have canned equivalents, although they are not identical in their ingredients or cooking techniques. Western Beans and Bean Puree have no canned substitutes. You can puree canned beans if you don't have time to cook your own.

Recipes in this section are written for stovetop preparation. Consequently, the finished beans have a rich flavor and aroma. Use your pressure cooker when the slow absorption and blending of flavors is not necessary to the finished dish and time is an important factor. See Pressure Cookers, pages 7 and 8.

All the directions for Basic Beans begin with 1 cup of dried beans. This yields a minimum of 2 cups of drained cooked beans. One cup of most bean types yields more than 2 cups, so be sure to measure the amount of cooked beans needed to make another recipe. If a recipe calls for more than 2 cups of cooked beans, double the basic recipe. Any extra beans can be refrigerated or frozen. If the recipe calls for less than 1 cup of cooked beans, prepare the full recipe and refrigerate or freeze what's left. See Leftovers and Freezing Cooked Beans, page 9.

When you cook any of these Basic Beans, plan ahead. Cook more than you immediately need. The beans you don't use can be stored in the refrigerator for at least 4 days—sometimes longer. Stock up by freezing for the future. Then on a day when you're rushed, the beans in the freezer will give you a head start for a quick meal.

For additional information on preparing and cooking beans, see pages 5 to 9.

Hard Water

If you consistently have problems cooking beans to the desired tenderness within the specified cooking times, it is possible you have *hard water*. Another sign of hard water is the appearance of a thick white or gray residue on the inside of your teakettle every time you boil water. This is caused by the presence of excessive amounts of certain minerals. High concentrations of these minerals interfere with chemical and physical changes that are supposed to occur in beans during soaking and cooking.

Some cooks suggest adding a small amount of baking soda to the cooking water to soften it. We don't recommend this because baking soda may give the beans a soapy flavor and its ability to improve the bean cooking process has not been proved. Amounts of baking soda over 1/8 teaspoon per cup of beans may destroy the thiamine (Vitamin B_1) in beans. Thiamine is a valuable nutrient and one reason why beans have a reputation for being nutritious.

If you have hard water, buy purified bottled drinking water—not distilled water—for soaking and cooking beans.

Cooked Beans

Use this basic recipe whenever cooked or canned beans are called for.

1 cup dried beans, see varieties listed below
Water for soaking
2-1/2 cups water

1 tablespoon vegetable oil
1 teaspoon salt

Sort and soak beans; see How To Prepare Dried Beans, pages 5 and 6. In a medium saucepan, combine drained soaked beans, 2-1/2 cups water, oil and salt. Bring to a boil; reduce heat. Cover and simmer until beans are tender; see table below. For pressure cooker directions, see pages 7 and 8. Makes about 2 cups of beans.

Cooked Lentils Or Peas

Lentils, split peas and black-eyed peas cook quickly and do not need to be soaked.

1 cup dried lentils, split peas or
    black-eyed peas
2-1/2 cups water

1 tablespoon vegetable oil
1 teaspoon salt

Sort and rinse lentils or peas. In a medium saucepan, combine rinsed lentils or peas, water, oil and salt. Bring to a boil; reduce heat. Cover and simmer until tender; see table below. For pressure cooker directions, see pages 7 and 8. Makes about 2 cups of lentils or peas.

Bean Cooking Times

Beans (soaked)	In A Saucepan	In A Pressure Cooker *
Black Beans	1 to 1-1/2 hours	5 to 8 minutes
Garbanzo Beans	1 to 1-1/2 hours	5 to 7 minutes
Great Northern Beans	1 to 1-1/2 hours	5 to 7 minutes
Lima Beans, Large	45 to 60 minutes	Not recommended
Lima Beans, Baby	1 hour	Not recommended
Pea Beans or Small White Beans	1 to 1-1/2 hours	5 to 8 minutes
Pink Beans	1 to 1-1/2 hours	6 to 8 minutes
Pinto Beans	1 to 1-1/2 hours	5 to 7 minutes
Red Beans	1 to 1-1/2 hours	6 to 8 minutes
Red Kidney Beans	1 to 1-1/2 hours	5 to 8 minutes
Soybeans	3 hours	12 to 15 minutes
Beans (not soaked)		
Black-Eyed Peas	1 to 1-1/2 hours	
Lentils	30 to 45 minutes	Not recommended
Split Peas, Green or Yellow	30 to 45 minutes	

*At 15 Pounds Pressure

Barbecue Beans

Red beans are particularly good with this smoky barbecue taste.

1 cup dried red beans, pinto beans,
   pink beans, kidney beans or lima beans
Water for soaking
2-1/2 cups water
2 slices bacon
1/4 cup chopped onion
1 garlic clove, minced
1/4 teaspoon salt

2 tablespoons ketchup
1 tablespoon chili sauce
1/2 tablespoon vinegar
1 tablespoon brown sugar
1/2 tablespoon prepared mustard
1/2 teaspoon salt
1/4 teaspoon pepper
Dash liquid smoke, if desired

Sort and soak beans; see How To Prepare Dried Beans, pages 5 and 6. In a medium saucepan, combine drained soaked beans and 2-1/2 cups water. In a small skillet, fry bacon until crisp. Drain on paper towels; crumble. Sauté onion and garlic in bacon drippings until onion is tender. Add sautéed onion mixture, crumbled bacon and salt to beans. Bring to a boil; reduce heat. Cover and simmer until beans are just tender, 1 to 1-1/2 hours. Drain, reserving cooking liquid. In a small bowl, combine 1/4 cup cooking liquid, ketchup, chili sauce, vinegar, brown sugar, mustard, salt, pepper and liquid smoke, if desired. Stir well. Add to beans, mixing well. Cover and simmer 30 minutes longer, adding more cooking liquid as needed. Makes about 2 cups of beans.

Variation

If cooking beans in a pressure cooker, read the instructions for Pressure Cookers, pages 7 and 8. Cook beans, 2-1/2 cups water, sautéed onion mixture, crumbled bacon and salt in cooker. When beans have cooked the shortest specified time, page 15, and pressure has been completely reduced, drain beans; reserve 1/4 cup cooking liquid. Combine reserved liquid and remaining ingredients. Stir mixture into beans. Replace lid without locking and cook without pressure 30 minutes.

Western Beans

With pinto beans, this recipe is the basis for famous Refried Beans, page 18.

1 cup dried pinto beans, red beans,
   red kidney beans or pink beans
Water for soaking
2-1/2 cups water
1 garlic clove, minced

1/3 cup chopped onion
1 tablespoon lard or bacon drippings
1 teaspoon salt
1/8 teaspoon pepper

Sort and soak beans, see How To Prepare Dried Beans, pages 5 and 6. In a medium saucepan, combine drained soaked beans, 2-1/2 cups water, garlic, onion, lard or bacon drippings, salt and pepper. Bring to a boil; reduce heat. Cover and simmer until beans are tender, 1 to 1/2 hours. Cool cooked bean mixture 1 hour, then reheat. Makes about 2 cups of beans.

Refried Beans

Traditional beans to serve with your favorite Mexican meal.

2 cups cooked Western Beans made with
    pinto beans, page 17
1/4 cup lard or shortening

1/2 cup shredded Monterey Jack cheese or
    Cheddar cheese
1/4 cup dairy sour cream, if desired

Drain beans, reserving cooking liquid. In a large skillet, heat lard or shortening until melted and very hot. Add cooked beans, mashing with a potato masher as they cook. Continue cooking and stirring until all lard or shortening is absorbed. Stir in reserved cooking liquid a small amount at a time for a thinner consistency. Add cheese. Cook and stir until cheese melts. Serve with a dollop of sour cream, if desired. Makes about 2 cups of beans.

Savory White Beans

Try them as a side dish or use them as a base for an appetizer, salad or casserole.

1 cup dried large or baby lima beans,
    Great Northern beans or pea beans
Water for soaking
2-1/2 cups water
2 chicken bouillon cubes

1 tablespoon vegetable oil
2 tablespoons chopped onion
1 garlic clove, minced
1/4 teaspoon salt

Sort and soak beans; see How To Prepare Dried Beans, pages 5 and 6. In a medium saucepan, combine drained soaked beans, 2-1/2 cups water and bouillon cubes. Heat oil in a small skillet. Sauté onion and garlic in oil until onion is tender but not browned. Add sautéed onion mixture to beans. Stir in salt. Bring beans to a boil; reduce heat. Cover and simmer until beans are tender; see Bean Cooking Times, page 15. Makes about 2 cups of beans.

Bean Puree

Bread and dessert recipes using this puree are on pages 148 to 157.

1 cup dried large lima beans,
    Great Northern beans or pinto beans
Water for soaking

2-1/2 cups water
1 teaspoon salt
1 tablespoon vegetable oil

Sort and soak beans; see How To Prepare Dried Beans, pages 5 and 6. In a medium saucepan, combine drained soaked beans, 2-1/2 cups water, salt and oil. Bring to a boil; reduce heat. Cover and simmer until beans are tender, 1 to 1-1/2 hours. Drain beans, reserving cooking liquid. Put 1 to 2 cups beans in blender with 1/4 cup to 1/2 cup reserved cooking liquid. Blend on medium speed until smooth, stopping blender occasionally to scrape sides and stir puree up from bottom. Bean mixture should circulate slowly. Makes about 2 cups of puree.

Chili Beans

Mildly spicy and very tasty.

1 cup dried red beans, pinto beans or
   pink beans
Water for soaking
2-1/2 cups water
1/2 teaspoon salt

1/4 cup chopped onion
1 tablespoon vegetable oil
1/2 cup Green Chili Salsa, page 69
1/2 to 1 teaspoon chili powder

Sort and soak beans; see How To Prepare Dried Beans, pages 5 and 6. In a medium saucepan, combine drained soaked beans, 2-1/2 cups water and salt. In a small skillet, sauté onion in oil until tender but not browned. Stir sautéed onion into beans. Bring to a boil; reduce heat. Cover and simmer until beans are tender, 1 to 1-1/2 hours. Prepare Green Chili Salsa. Drain beans, reserving 1/4 to 1/2 cup cooking liquid. In a small bowl, combine 1/4 cup cooking liquid, Green Chili Salsa and chili powder. Stir salsa mixture into beans. Simmer beans 30 minutes longer, stirring frequently. Add more cooking liquid if needed. Makes about 2 cups of beans.

Variation

If cooking beans in a pressure cooker, read the instructions for Pressure Cookers, pages 7 and 8. Do not add Green Chili Salsa and chili powder until beans have cooked the shortest specified time, page 15, and pressure has been completely reduced. Drain beans, reserving 1/4 to 1/2 cup cooking liquid. Then stir salsa and chili powder into reserved cooking liquid. Add mixture to beans. Replace lid without locking and cook without pressure 30 minutes.

How To Make Bean Puree

1/Put cooked beans and some cooking liquid in the blender. Blend on medium speed until smooth; stop occasionally to scrape down sides and stir beans up from the bottom.

2/Bean Puree should be smooth in consistency. Use it immediately or refrigerate 2 to 3 days. It will thicken as it cools. Freeze in an airtight container to store up to 6 weeks.

Appetizers, Snacks & Sandwiches

Appetizers stimulate not only the appetite, but also warmth and good feelings. Those using beans are also tasty, unusual and nutritious. So don't serve plain chips and dip. Try bite-size sausages or meatballs with Spicy Dip or fill a basket or wooden bowl with fresh raw vegetables to go with Herbed Lima Dip.

Keep Toasted Bean Snacks in a cannister to serve friends who drop in—that is if you can keep them in a canister! Crunchy and nut-like, toasted beans can be spiced with onion, garlic or chili seasoning. In our house, they disappear almost as fast as we make them!

Many of the appetizers and sandwiches begin with cooked beans. You'll discover that they are a great way to use leftover beans. Set aside some Texas Chili With Beans, page 86, to make Baked Chili Sandwiches. Prepare extra Refried Beans, page 18, so you can serve Range Fire with corn chips or tortilla chips.

TOFU

Tòfu, or bean curd, is a high-protein food made from soybeans. It is low in fat and calories and contains no cholesterol. Tofu looks like cheese and is made by a similar process. It is cream-colored and has a bland flavor. Because it readily absorbs flavors from other foods, tofu is a useful ingredient in a variety of dishes. We feature it here in Tofu-Avocado Dip and Tofu Salad Sandwiches.

You can buy tofu in Oriental food stores, health food stores and some grocery stores or supermarkets. It is usually in a solid cake covered with liquid and packaged in plastic containers. It may also be crumbled in liquid. Some stores sell it from bulk. Tofu will keep 4 to 5 days in the refrigerator. Drain off the liquid each day and cover the tofu again with fresh cool water.

CHOW CHOW TIPS

Brown sugar in Chow Chow causes the vegetables, especially cauliflower, to darken slightly. However, Chow Chow made with brown sugar has a superior flavor.

When you make Chow Chow or any other pickled vegetables, **do not cut down on the amount of vinegar called for.** Less vinegar may result in improper preservation of the vegetables and increase the opportunity for toxins to develop. If the flavor is too sharp, add more brown sugar or other sweetener.

Deliciously Refreshing Lunch
Deli Delights, page 31
Garden Vegetable Soup, page 51
Old-Fashioned Rice Pudding
Crisp Coconut Cookies

Guests For Dinner
Tangy Lima Bean Appetizer, page 28
Crown Roast Of Lamb
With
Herbed Bread & Mushroom Stuffing
Honey-Lemon Beans, page 129
Marinated Tomato Slices
Cloverleaf Rolls
Coffee Ice Cream Pie

Egg Roll Platter

Using a warming tray guarantees the egg rolls and sauce will stay warm.

1 cup Bean Puree made with Great Northern
 beans, page 18
3 (6-oz.) pkgs. frozen bite-size egg rolls
 (36 egg rolls)
2 tablespoons chopped onion
1 tablespoon butter or margarine

1 tablespoon all-purpose flour
1 cup milk
1/4 cup prepared mustard
1 teaspoon Worcestershire sauce
1/2 teaspoon salt
2 to 4 drops Tabasco sauce

Prepare Bean Puree. Preheat oven to 400°F (205°C). Put egg rolls on a baking sheet. Bake 12 to 15 minutes, turning once. In a medium saucepan, sauté onion in butter or margarine until tender but not browned. Add flour; stir until blended. Stir in Bean Puree. Add milk, mustard, Worcestershire sauce, salt and Tabasco sauce; stir until smooth. Bring to a boil over medium heat. Keep warm, adding water if necessary to maintain consistency. Pour sauce into a small bowl and place in the center of a platter. Surround bowl with hot egg rolls. Refrigerate or freeze extra sauce. Makes 10 to 12 servings.

Variation

Deep-Fried Vegetable Platter: Substitute 3 (9-ounce) packages frozen deep-fried zucchini or 3 (7-ounce) packages frozen deep-fried eggplant for egg rolls. Bake in preheated 400°F (205°C) oven 10 to 15 minutes. Surround bowl of mustard sauce with fried vegetables. Makes 8 to 10 servings.

Black-Eyed Fritters

Subtly flavored fritters are perfect with Creole Dipping Sauce for a cocktail buffet.

1-1/2 cups drained cooked black-eyed peas,
 page 15, or 1 (15-oz.) can black-eyed peas,
 drained
Creole Dipping Sauce, page 71
Oil for deep-frying
1 slice bacon
2 tablespoons finely chopped onion

1 garlic clove, minced
1 egg, beaten
1/3 cup unsifted all-purpose flour
1/4 teaspoon salt
1/8 teaspoon pepper
Pinch of dried leaf thyme

Prepare black-eyed peas and Creole Dipping Sauce. Heat oil in a deep-fryer or large heavy pot to 350°F (175°C). At this temperature a 1-inch cube of bread will turn golden brown in 65 seconds. In a medium bowl, mash black-eyed peas with a potato masher until chunky. In a small skillet, fry bacon until crisp. Drain on paper towels. Sauté onion and garlic in bacon drippings until onion is tender but not browned. Combine sautéed onion mixture with mashed black-eyed peas. Stir in egg. Add flour, salt, pepper and thyme; mix well. Drop by teaspoonfuls into hot oil. Fry until golden brown, 3 to 5 minutes. Drain on paper towels. Serve with warm Creole Dipping Sauce. Makes about 36 fritters.

Tofu-Avocado Dip

Mild-flavored soybean curd or tofu *will keep 4 or 5 days in the refrigerator.*

1/2 lb. tofu, drained
1 medium avocado, peeled, mashed
2 tablespoons dairy sour cream or mayonnaise
1/2 teaspoon salt

1 teaspoon lemon juice
1/2 tablespoon finely chopped or grated onion
4 drops Tabasco sauce
Cayenne pepper to taste

In a medium bowl, stir tofu to break up the curd. Add avocado, sour cream or mayonnaise, salt, lemon juice, onion, Tabasco sauce and cayenne pepper. Mix well. Refrigerate at least 1 hour before serving. Makes about 1-1/2 cups of dip.

Spicy Dip

Spear the sausages or meatballs with brightly colored cocktail picks.

1 cup Bean Puree made with
   Great Northern beans, page 18
1/4 cup chopped onion
1 garlic clove, minced
1 tablespoon bacon drippings

1/2 cup chopped tomato, fresh or canned
1/8 teaspoon pepper
1 teaspoon chili powder
1 lb. cocktail sausages, cooked, or
   24 Yeoman's Meatballs, page 136

Prepare Bean Puree. In a small saucepan, sauté onion and garlic in bacon drippings until onion is tender but not browned. Add Bean Puree, tomato, pepper and chili powder. Mix well. Bring to a boil. Keep warm in a chafing dish, adding water if necessary to maintain the consistency. Serve with cocktail sausages or meatballs for dipping. Makes 1 cup.

Cheese & Bacon Spread

Use this hearty dish as a dip or spread for toast or crackers.

2 cups cooked Great Northern beans,
   page 15, or 1 (15-oz.) can cannellini
   beans
3 slices bacon

2 oz. bulk pork sausage
1/4 teaspoon Tabasco sauce
1/2 cup shredded sharp Cheddar cheese

Prepare beans; drain, reserving 1/3 to 1/2 cup liquid. Add water if necessary. Mash beans with a potato masher in a medium bowl, adding liquid as necessary for a spreadable consistency. In a small skillet, fry bacon until crisp. Drain on paper towels; crumble. Pour bacon drippings from skillet and set aside. Fry sausage in the same skillet, breaking up meat. Drain drippings from skillet. Add sausage and Tabasco sauce to mashed beans; mix well. Return 2 tablespoons bacon drippings to skillet and fry bean mixture 10 minutes, stirring occasionally. Preheat oven to broil. Place beans in an ovenproof serving dish or individual ramkins. Top with grated cheese. Broil until cheese melts. Makes 2 cups of spread.

Chili Cheese Dip, page 26, is top right. On the tray, clockwise, is Tofu-Avocado Dip, opposite; Toasted Bean Snacks, page 28; and Boston Tea Sandwiches, page 30.

Nachos

Jalapeño peppers are fiery hot! For a milder taste, use canned green chilies.

1 cup Refried Beans, page 18, or
   1 cup canned refried beans
Oil for frying
6 corn tortillas
1 tablespoon finely chopped onion

2 teaspoons butter or margarine
1/2 teaspoon salt
1 cup shredded Longhorn cheese
6 canned small whole jalapeño peppers
   washed, seeded, cut in quarters

Prepare beans. Heat about 1/4 inch oil in a medium skillet. Cut tortillas into quarters. Fry a few quarters at a time in hot oil until crisp. Drain on paper towels. Preheat oven to 375°F (190°C). In a small saucepan, sauté onion in butter or margarine until tender but not browned. Add refried beans and salt. Heat until bubbly, stirring occasionally. Arrange tortilla chips on a baking sheet. Top each chip with a dab of beans, a pinch of grated cheese and a piece of jalapeño pepper. Bake 10 minutes or until cheese melts. Serve warm. Makes 24 nachos.

Lentil Burgers

If you want to break the hamburger habit, try this!

3/4 cup dried lentils
2 cups water
1 teaspoon salt
1/4 cup uncooked brown rice
1 cup fresh fine breadcrumbs, page 102
1/2 cup chopped walnuts
1/4 cup finely chopped onion
1/8 teaspoon pepper

1/4 teaspoon dried leaf basil
1/4 cup wheat germ
2 tablespoons vegetable oil
2 pita bread rounds
2 cups shredded lettuce
1 cup diced fresh tomato
Buttermilk-style salad dressing

Sort and rinse lentils. Combine lentils, water and salt in a medium saucepan. Bring to a boil. Stir in rice; reduce heat. Cover and simmer 45 minutes. Mash lentils and rice together in a medium bowl. Stir in breadcrumbs, walnuts, onion, pepper and basil; mix well. Put wheat germ in a shallow bowl. Shape lentil mixture into 4 patties. Place each patty in wheat germ to coat; turn to coat other side. Heat oil in a large skillet. Fry patties until browned. Turn once to brown other side. Cut each pita bread round in half and carefully separate sides of bread to make a pocket. Fill each pocket with a cooked patty and some lettuce and tomato. Drizzle with dressing. Makes 4 servings.

Miniature Croquettes

Bite size croquettes with a cheese center are fun and different.

2 cups drained cooked black beans, page 15
1 tablespoon butter or margarine
2 tablespoons chopped onion
1 teaspoon salt
1/4 teaspoon oregano
2 tablespoons freshly grated Parmesan cheese

4 oz. bulk Monterey Jack cheese
1 egg
1 tablespoon water
1/2 cup fresh fine breadcrumbs, page 102
1/2 cup freshly grated Parmesan cheese
Oil for deep-frying

Prepare beans and mash to a chunky consistency. In a small skillet, sauté onion in butter or margarine until tender but not browned. Add sautéed onion, salt, oregano and 2 tablespoons Parmesan cheese to beans; mix well. Cut Monterey Jack cheese into 32 cubes. In a small bowl, beat egg and water. In a pie plate, combine breadcrumbs and 1/2 cup Parmesan cheese. Heat oil in a deep-fryer or large heavy pot to 350°F (175°C). At this temperature, a 1-inch cube of bread will turn golden brown in 65 seconds. To make croquettes, place a cube of cheese in the center of a tablespoon of bean mixture. Shape bean mixture into a ball around cheese cube, being sure cheese is completely covered. Roll croquette in breadcrumbs, dip in egg mixture and then into breadcrumbs again. Fry in hot oil until golden. Drain on paper towels. Keep warm until all are fried. Serve warm. Makes 32 bite-size croquettes.

How To Make Miniature Croquettes

1/Push a cheese cube into 1 tablespoon of bean mixture. Mold bean mixture around cheese. Completely cover cheese so it will not melt out of croquette while frying.

2/Roll cheese-filled balls in Parmesan breadcrumbs, dip in beaten egg and roll in breadcrumbs again. Deep-fry croquettes until the coating is a toasty brown.

Soybean Spread

Spread this delicious wholesome blend on cocktail crackers.

1 cup drained cooked soybeans, page 15
2 tablespoons chopped onion
1/2 tablespoon butter or margarine
2 tablespoons tomato sauce

2 tablespoons chopped black olives
1 tablespoon sesame seeds
1 tablespoon chopped fresh parsley
1/2 teaspoon salt

Prepare soybeans. In a small bowl, mash soybeans with a potato masher until smooth. In a small skillet, sauté onion in butter or margarine until tender but not browned. Add tomato sauce, olives and sautéed onions to soybeans. Toast sesame seeds by stirring constantly in a small heavy skillet over medium heat until lightly browned; watch carefully because the seeds burn very easily. Add toasted seeds, parsley and salt to soybean mixture; mix well. Makes 1 cup of spread.

Chili Cheese Dip *Photo on page 23.*

Keep the dip warm in a chafing dish, fondue pot or crock pot; serve with tortilla chips.

4 cups drained cooked kidney or pinto beans,
    page 14, or 2 (15-oz.) cans kidney or
    pinto beans, drained
1 cup Green Chili Salsa, page 69

1 lb. process American cheese
1/2 lb. ground beef
1/2 cup chopped onion
1 teaspoon salt

Prepare beans and Green Chili Salsa. Melt cheese in a double boiler over hot water, stirring occasionally. In a medium skillet, brown beef with onion until meat is no longer pink and onion is softened. Drain excess fat from meat mixture. Add Green Chili Salsa, salt and beans to meat mixture; mix well. Cover and cook over low heat about 10 minutes until mixture is bubbly. Stir bean mixture into melted cheese. Serve warm. Makes about 7 cups of dip.

Range Fire

Jalapeño peppers make a fiery dip. Serve it warm with plenty of corn chips or tortilla chips.

2 cups Refried Beans, page 18, or
    1 (17-oz.) can refried beans
1/4 cup finely chopped onion
2 tablespoons butter or margarine
2 canned medium jalapeño peppers, washed,
    seeded, finely chopped, or 1 (4-oz.) can
    diced or chopped green chilies

1/2 cup shredded Cheddar cheese
1/2 cup shredded Monterey Jack cheese

Prepare beans. In a medium saucepan, sauté onion in butter or margarine until tender but not browned. Add beans and jalapeño peppers or green chilies. Stir frequently over low heat until bubbly. Just before serving, add cheeses. Heat and stir until cheeses are melted. Makes 2 cups of dip.

Green Bean Chow Chow *Photo on page 68.*

Serve on an appetizer tray with carrot and celery sticks. Chow Chow Tips are on page 20.

1 lb. fresh green beans	2-1/2 cups water
1 small cauliflower, cut into small flowerets	2-1/2 cups cider vinegar
1 cucumber, peeled, chopped	1 cup packed brown sugar
1/2 cup chopped green pepper	1 teaspoon turmeric
1 medium onion, sliced	1 teaspoon dry mustard
1 cup sliced celery	1/2 teaspoon ground cloves
4 tablespoons salt	1/2 teaspoon black pepper

Stem green beans and cut into small pieces. In a 3-quart casserole, layer green beans, cauliflowerets, cucumber, green pepper, onion and celery, sprinkling each layer with salt. Refrigerate at least 24 hours. Drain. Wash five 1-pint canning jars, lids and metal rings in hot, soapy water; rinse well. Sterilize jars by placing them in a large pot of boiling water. Cover and boil 20 minutes. Follow manufacturer's instructions for preparing jar lids and rings. In a 4-quart pot, combine vinegar, water, brown sugar, turmeric, dry mustard, cloves and black pepper. Bring to a boil. Add drained vegetables. Cover and simmer 10 minutes. Remove jars 1 at a time from boiling water when ready to fill. With a slotted spoon, pack hot vegetables in hot sterilized jars, leaving slightly more than 1/2 inch at top of each jar. Pour boiling vinegar mixture into jars to cover vegetables, leaving at least 1/2 inch at top of each jar. Seal jars following manufacturer's instructions. Place on a rack in a deep pot. Pour boiling water in pot to cover tops of jars by 2 inches. Cover pot. Quickly bring water to a boil again. Process, or boil, 5 minutes from the time the water boils gently and steadily, or adjust time according to altitude. Remove jars. Cool away from drafts. When cool, check all seals. Lids should be tight and slightly concave. If lid gives when pressed in center, it has not sealed. Refrigerate unsealed jars and use within 2 or 3 weeks. Store sealed jars in a cool dark place. If lid has lost its seal, or popped out in center, or if vegetables have a bad odor or are mushy or moldy when jar is opened, discard without tasting. Let stand 2 weeks for flavors to develop. Makes about 5 pints of relish.

Herbed Lima Dip

Look for Bon Appètit seasoning on the spice shelves in your supermarket.

1/3 cup water	1/2 cup dairy sour cream
1/2 teaspoon salt	2 teaspoons dried dill weed
1 (10-oz.) pkg. frozen baby lima beans	2 teaspoons Bon Appètit seasoning
1/3 cup finely chopped onion	1/2 teaspoon curry powder
1 garlic clove, minced	Assorted raw vegetable dippers
1/2 cup mayonnaise	

In a medium saucepan, bring water and salt to a boil. Add frozen lima beans, onion and garlic. Reduce heat. Cover and simmer 5 minutes. Break beans apart with a fork. Cover and cook until beans are tender, about 10 minutes longer. Put bean mixture with cooking liquid in blender container. Blend until smooth. Add mayonnaise, sour cream, dill weed, Bon Appètit seasoning and curry powder. Blend to mix well. Refrigerate several hours or overnight. Serve with raw vegetable dippers such as carrot and celery sticks, cauliflowerets and green onions. Makes 2 cups of dip.

Toasted Bean Snacks   *Photo on page 23.*

Store this crunchy snack in an airtight container or make up several gift containers.

2 cups dried soybeans
Water for soaking
2 teaspoons vegetable oil

1 teaspoon salt
1 teaspoon garlic salt

Sort and soak beans, See How To Prepare Dried Beans, pages 5 and 6. Drain beans; discard soak water. Preheat oven to 200°F (95°C). Spread soaked beans on a jelly-roll pan or 13" x 9" baking pan. Bake 2-1/2 hours. Remove beans from oven. Sprinkle with oil; toss to coat all beans. Return beans to oven and bake 1/2 hour longer. Remove from oven. Mix salt and garlic salt in a small bowl. Sprinkle beans with salt mixture; mix well. Makes 2 cups of toasted beans.

Variations

Substitute 2 teaspoons onion powder or 2 teaspoons chili powder for 1 teaspoon garlic salt.

Use 2 cups drained cooked garbanzo beans. Follow directions above. After toasting, toss with 1 teaspoon butter or margarine and salt mixture. Do not use canned garbanzo beans.

Tangy Lima Bean Appetizer

If you're serving buffet-style, pile the lima beans on spinach leaves on a large platter.

1 cup dried large lima beans
Water for soaking
2-1/2 cups water
1 teaspoon salt
2 garlic cloves, minced
3 tablespoons vegetable oil

1 carrot, sliced
1/2 green pepper, diced
2 tablespoons chopped fresh parsley
Pinch of dried dill weed
Fresh spinach leaves, washed, stems removed
1 lemon, cut in 6 wedges

Sort and soak beans. See How To Prepare Dried Beans, pages 5 and 6. Drain beans; discard soak water. In a medium saucepan, combine soaked beans, 2-1/2 cups water and salt. Bring to a boil. Reduce heat. Cover and simmer until beans are just tender, about 45 minutes. In a small skillet, sauté garlic in oil 1 minute. Add carrot and green pepper. Sauté 2 minutes longer. Stir in parsley and dill weed. Cook and stir 3 minutes. Add sautéed vegetable mixture to beans. Simmer 15 minutes longer until beans are very tender but still retain their shapes. Cool to room temperature. Arrange spinach leaves on 6 small plates. Spoon bean mixture over spinach leaves. Garnish with lemon wedges to squeeze over beans. Makes 6 servings.

When you cook bacon, don't discard the bacon drippings. Refrigerate them in a tin can with a plastic lid and use them whenever bacon drippings are called for.

Huevos Rancheros Burritos

For tostadas, fry 6-inch tortillas in oil. Serve them flat, topped with beans, eggs and garnishes.

2 cups Refried Beans, page 18, or
  1 (17-oz.) can refried beans
1 cup Green Chili Salsa, page 69, or
  1 (8-oz.) can green chili salsa
2 green onions, sliced
1/4 cup chopped green pepper
1 tablespoon butter or margarine

1/2 cup shredded Monterey Jack cheese
4 (10-inch) flour tortillas
3 tablespoons vegetable oil
4 eggs
2 medium tomatoes, diced
1/2 cup shredded Longhorn cheese
Shredded lettuce

Prepare Refried Beans and salsa. In a medium saucepan, sauté green onions and green pepper in butter or margarine until tender but not browned. Add Refried Beans. Warm over medium heat 10 minutes, stirring frequently to prevent sticking. Stir in Monterey Jack cheese. Cover and simmer until cheese melts. To warm tortillas, wrap in a clean towel and steam on a rack in a covered saucepan, or preheat oven to 350°F (175°C), wrap tortillas in foil and warm in oven 15 minutes. Heat oil in a large heavy skillet. Fry eggs in oil until whites are set. For each burrito, place 1 tortilla on a plate. Spread about 1/2 cup beans 1/2 inch thick on half of the tortilla. Place a fried egg on top of beans. Sprinkle with about 1/4 cup salsa, 1/4 of the diced tomato and 2 tablespoons shredded Longhorn cheese. Fold over edge of tortilla next to filling. Fold over the 2 sides envelope-fashion. Roll up tortilla. Surround burrito with shredded lettuce. Top with a spoonful of salsa. Makes 4 burritos.

How To Make Huevos Rancheros Burritos

1/Spread bean mixture on a warm flour tortilla. Cover about half the tortilla, leaving a 1/2-inch margin around the covered side. Place a fried egg on beans. Top with Green Chili Salsa, diced tomato and shredded cheese.

2/Fold tortilla edge with beans over the egg. Fold in each side envelope-fashion; roll up the tortilla. Place rolled tortilla seam-side down on plate. Surround with shredded lettuce. Garnish with salsa and hot peppers, if desired.

Dilly Beans

Altitude adjustments for canning can be obtained from your local extension service.

2 lbs. small tender fresh green beans	1 tablespoon dill seed
Boiling water	4 garlic cloves
2 cups water	4 sprigs fresh dill, stems removed, or
2 cups cider vinegar	1 teaspoon dried dill weed
1/4 cup salt	4 red pepper pods, if desired

Stem green beans and trim so they will just fit lengthwise into 1-pint canning jars. Wash four 1-pint jars, lids and metal rings in hot soapy water; rinse well. Sterilize jars by placing them in a large pot of boiling water. Cover and boil 20 minutes. Follow manufacturer's instructions for preparing jar-lids and rings. Put green beans in a large saucepan. Add enough boiling water to cover beans by 2 inches. Simmer 10 minutes. In a medium saucepan, combine 2 cups water, vinegar, salt and dill seed. Bring to a boil. Cover and simmer 5 minutes. Remove jars 1 at a time from boiling water when ready to fill. Drain green beans and pack in hot sterilized jars, leaving slightly more tthan 1/2 inch at top of each jar. To each jar add a garlic clove, a dill sprig and a red pepper pod, if desired. Strain hot vinegar mixture into jars to cover beans, leaving at least 1/2 inch at top of each jar. Seal jars following manufacturer's instructions. Place on a rack in a deep pot. Pour boiling water in pot to cover top of jars by 2 inches. Cover pot. Quickly bring water to a boil again. Process, or boil, 5 minutes from the time the water boils gently and steadily or adjust time according to altitude. Remove jars. Cool away from drafts. When cool, check all seals. Lids should be tight and slightly concave. If lid gives when pressed in center, it has not sealed. Refrigerate unsealed jars and use within 2 or 3 weeks. Store sealed jars in a cool dark place. Let stand 2 weeks before using for the flavors to develop. If lid has lost its seal, or popped out in the center, or if vegetables have a bad odor or are mushy or moldy when the jar is opened, discard without tasting. Makes 4 pints of pickled beans.

Variation

Dilled Green Beans & Okra: Use 1 pound green beans and 1 pound fresh okra. Cut beans the same size as okra. Wash okra and trim ends. Cook beans as directed above. Add okra. Cook 1 minute longer. Drain and pack in hot, sterilized jars. Prepare vinegar mixture as directed above. Pour over beans and okra leaving at least 1/2 inch at top of jars. Process in boiling water as above.

Boston Tea Sandwiches *Photo on page 23.*

Make fancy luncheon sandwiches with traditional baked beans and brown bread.

4 slices bacon	2 tablespoons chili sauce
1 (16-oz.) can baked beans	1 (3-oz.) pkg. cream cheese
2 tablespoons finely chopped onion	1 (16-oz.) can Boston brown bread

In a medium skillet, fry bacon until crisp. Drain on paper towels. Combine beans, onion and chili sauce in a small saucepan. Cover and cook over low heat 5 minutes, stirring occasionally. Cool to room temperature. In a small bowl, whip cream cheese with electric mixer on medium speed until light. Cut bread into 10 thick slices. Generously spread each slice with cream cheese and top with a mound of baked beans. Crumble bacon over each sandwich. Makes 10 sandwiches.

Capistrano Sandwiches

Salad olives are more economical than regular pimiento-stuffed olives.

2 cups drained cooked garbanzo beans,
    page 15, or 1 (15-oz.) can garbanzo
    beans, drained
3 to 4 tablespoons Sesame Seed Dressing,
    page 73

1 medium avocado, peeled, diced
1/4 cup sliced pimiento-stuffed olives
1 cup torn fresh spinach leaves
4 pita bread rounds

Prepare beans and Sesame Seed Dressing. In a medium bowl, combine beans, avocado, olives, spinach and Sesame Seed Dressing. Toss gently. Cut each pita bread round in half and carefully separate sides of bread to make a pocket. Stuff each pocket with bean mixture. Serve immediately. Makes 4 servings.

Baked Chili Sandwiches

Shredding cheese is easy and quick if you use the coarse side of your grater.

2 cups Texas Chili With Beans, page 86, or
    1 (16-oz.) can chili with beans
9 slices bread
2 tablespoons butter or margarine

1 cup shredded Cheddar cheese
4 eggs
2-1/2 cups milk
1/2 teaspoon salt

Prepare chili. Spread one side of 6 slices of bread with butter or margarine. In a 12" x 7-1/2" baking pan, arrange bread slices buttered-side down in a single layer. Spoon chili over bread; sprinkle with grated cheese. Cut remaining 3 slices of bread in half diagonally. Arrange bread slices on top of chili. Beat eggs in a medium bowl. Add milk and salt; stir. Pour egg mixture over sandwiches. Refrigerate 1 hour or longer. Preheat oven to 350°F (175°C). Bake until puffed and golden brown, 45 minutes to 1 hour. With a spatula, cut between bottom bread slices and serve. Makes 6 sandwiches.

Deli Delights

Cut julienne strips, or matchsticks, with a sharp knife on a cutting board or in your food processor.

1 cup drained cooked garbanzo beans,
    page 15, or 1 (8-oz.) can garbanzo beans,
    drained
4 to 6 tablespoons Italian Salad Dressing,
    page 66
1/2 cup julienne strips Swiss cheese

1/2 cup julienne strips Cheddar cheese
1/2 cup julienne strips cooked chicken
1/2 cup julienne strips ham
1 green onion, chopped
4 pita bread rounds

Prepare beans and Italian Salad Dressing. In a medium bowl, combine all ingredients except pita bread. Toss gently to coat with dressing. May be refrigerated overnight. Cut each pita bread round in half and carefully separate sides of bread to make a pocket. Stuff each pocket with filling. Makes 4 servings.

Monterey Grilled Sandwiches

Serve with a salad of avocado wedges, sliced tomatoes and shredded lettuce.

2 cups Refried Beans, page 18, or
   1 (17-oz.) can refried beans
1 tablespoon butter or margarine
1 tablespoon finely chopped onion
2 tablespoons finely chopped green pepper
1 teaspoon chili powder

12 slices bread
6 tablespoons butter or margarine
6 oz. Monterey Jack cheese, sliced
1 (4-oz.) can whole green chilies, seeded,
   cut in strips

Prepare beans. Melt butter or margarine in a medium saucepan. Add onion and green pepper. Stir constantly over medium heat until onion is tender but not browned. Stir in refried beans and chili powder. Cook over low heat 10 minutes. Spread one side of each slice of bread with butter or margarine. Heat a large heavy skillet or griddle over medium heat. Place bread slices buttered-side down on hot skillet. Place a cheese slice on each slice of bread. Spread each cheese slice with about 1/3 cup bean mixture and top with another cheese slice. Arrange green chili strips on cheese. Top with remaining bread, buttered-side up. Grill sandwiches on each side until golden brown. Serve warm. Makes 6 servings.

Tofu Salad Sandwiches

Look for tofu *in the refrigerator cases of an oriental or health food store.*

12 slices Pinto Wheat Bread, page 149, or
   whole-wheat bread
2 cups fresh lentil sprouts or alfalfa sprouts
1 lb. tofu
1/4 cup mayonnaise
1 tablespoon prepared mustard
1 teaspoon Worcestershire sauce
1/2 teaspoon salt

1/8 teaspoon ground cumin
1/8 teaspoon ground turmeric
1/4 teaspoon paprika
1 green onion, minced
1/4 cup shredded carrot
1/4 cup minced celery
2 tablespoons minced green pepper

If making your own bread, prepare Pinto Wheat Bread. Prepare sprouts. In a medium bowl, crumble tofu with a fork or pastry blender to small lumps. Stir in mayonnaise, mustard and Worcestershire sauce. Sprinkle salt, cumin, turmeric and paprika over salad mixture. Stir well. Add green onion, carrot, celery and green pepper; stir. For each sandwich, place a mound of salad on a slice of bread. Spread to edges. Top salad with a generous layer of sprouts. Place another slice of bread on sprouts. Cut sandwiches in half to make them easier to eat. Makes 6 sandwiches.

Bean Bundles

Bundles rise during baking and will open at their seams if they are not securely sealed.

1 (8-oz.) can refrigerated crescent rolls
1 cup baked beans such as Boston Baked
   Beans, page 83, Southern-Style Baked
   Beans, page 84, or canned baked beans

2 tablespoons bottled barbecue sauce
1/2 teaspoon Worcestershire sauce
4 smoky sausage links or hot dogs

Preheat oven to 375°F (190°C). Separate crescent roll dough into 4 rectangles. Firmly press remaining diagonal perforations to seal rectangles and prevent separation during baking. In a small bowl, combine beans, barbecue sauce and Worcestershire sauce. With a fork or potato masher, mash beans to a chunky consistency. Spread rectangle with about 1/4 cup bean mixture, leaving a 1/4-inch margin. Place a sausage link or hot dog lengthwise in the middle of each rectangle. Pull up both sides of rectangle; pinch to close. With a serrated knife, cut each roll into 4 slices. Place cut-side down on an ungreased baking sheet. Bake in preheated oven 15 to 20 minutes until golden brown. Cool slightly. Remove from baking sheet. Serve warm. Makes 16 bundles.

How To Make Bean Bundles

1/After you have thoroughly sealed the perforations on the dough, spread dough with bean mixture, leaving a 1/4-inch margin.

2/Place a sausage or hot dog in the middle of bean-covered dough. Carefully raise both long sides of dough and pinch together. Using a serrated knife to slice the Bean Bundles will help prevent the bean mixture from squeezing out.

Chili Sizes

A beef patty and chili beans on a bun is a California specialty called a chili size.

2 cups Chili Beans, page 19, or
   1 (16-oz.) can chili beans
1 lb. lean ground beef
1/2 cup fresh fine breadcrumbs, page 102
1 egg, beaten
1 teaspoon salt

Pepper to taste
1/4 teaspoon ground cumin
4 hamburger buns
2 tablespoons butter or margarine
1/2 cup shredded Longhorn cheese

Prepare Chili Beans; keep warm. In a medium bowl, combine ground beef, breadcrumbs, egg, salt, pepper and cumin; mix well. Shape into 4 patties. Preheat oven to broil. Fry patties in a large heavy skillet over medium-high heat until browned on both sides and barely pink in center. Split hamburger buns; spread with butter or margarine. Toast buns under broiler. For each sandwich, place toasted bun open on a plate. Put beef patty on bun. Top with about 1/2 cup warm Chili Beans. Sprinkle with shredded cheese. Makes 4 sandwiches.

Oriental Pocket Sandwiches

Look for pita bread, *or* pocket bread, *in the frozen baked goods section of your supermarket.*

1 cup mung bean sprouts
1 chicken breast, boned, skinned,
   cut in strips, page 117
1 celery rib, diced
1/2 cup chopped onion
1 cup fresh or frozen snow peas,
   cut in thirds
1/3 cup sliced water chestnuts
1/2 teaspoon salt
2 tablespoons chicken broth

1 tablespoon dry white wine or
   additional chicken broth
2 teaspoons soy sauce
1/4 teaspoon sugar
1/8 teaspoon ground ginger
1 teaspoon cornstarch
1 tablespoon cold water
4 pita bread rounds
2 tablespoons sliced almonds

Prepare bean sprouts. Heat oil in a wok or large heavy skillet. Add chicken, celery and onion. Stir until chicken begins to turn white. Add snow peas, water chestnuts and salt. Stir in chicken broth, wine or additional chicken broth, soy sauce, sugar and ginger. Cover and simmer 5 minutes. Stir in bean sprouts. In a small bowl, combine cornstarch and cold water. Stir into chicken mixture. Stir constantly over medium heat until liquid thickens and boils. Cut each pita bread round in half and carefully separate sides of bread to make a pocket. Spoon chicken mixture into pockets. Sprinkle filling with almonds. Makes 4 servings.

Soups

Endless flavors and textures are possible in bean soups because of the variety of beans, meats, vegetables, herbs and seasonings that can be combined. Use the same bean, but vary the meat, vegetable or flavorings and you have a completely different soup. For example, Chick Pea & Sausage Soup using sausage with garbanzo beans is distinctly different from Spanish Chicken Soup using chicken with garbanzo beans.

Whether a soup should be thick or thin is a matter of preference. If you want the finished soup to be thinner, add a small amount of water or other liquid used to prepare the recipe. Any creamy soup, such as Bean Corn Chowder or Mixed Bean Chowder, or one with a thick bean base, like Hungarian Bean Soup or Capitol Hill Special, can be thickened in one of two ways:

If the cooked bean soup cools and is then reheated, the liquid will thicken because the natural starch in the beans has been incorporated into it. The cooler the soup becomes, the thicker it will be when it is reheated. This is one reason why bean soups are better the day after they are cooked.

A faster method is to remove some beans from the pot—not more than 1 cup. Puree them in your blender and stir the puree into the still simmering soup. Repeat until the soup is as thick as you want it. This method makes the starch in the pureed beans immediately available for thickening.

BROTH OR BOUILLON?

Homemade beef or chicken broth or stock is best to use in preparing beans and bean dishes. If you don't have homemade stock or broth in your freezer, canned broth and bouillon cubes or granules are good substitutes.

Canned broth can be used full strength from the can. It's made from liquid in which beef or chicken has cooked. Flavor extracts, chicken fat and flavor enhancers have been added. Broth has a rich natural flavor which makes it an excellent choice as a base for soups, stocks, sauces and gravies.

Bouillon can be purchased as cubes or granules to dissolve in boiling water. It is made from beef or chicken extracts, flavor enhancers and seasonings. Bouillon is very salty and has a distinctive flavor. Use it to give a flavor boost to bean soups and stews or to add flavor to plain cooked beans.

Light Lunch
Ginger Soup, page 41
Spinach & Sprouts, page 56
Sesame Crackers
Fruit Cup
Buttery Pecan Cookies

Back-To-School Dinner
Split Pea Soup With Mushrooms,
page 46
Grilled Pork Chops
Cinnamon Applesauce
Pilgrim Pudding, page 122
Tossed Bacon, Spinach & Tomato Salad
Harvest Pie, page 151

Vegetable Beef Soup

Barley, sometimes called pearl barley, *adds nutrition to soups, cereals, breads and puddings.*

1 cup dried baby lima beans
Water for soaking
1 lb. beef shanks or meaty soup bones
9 cups water
4 beef bouillon cubes
1 teaspoon salt
6 peppercorns
1 celery rib with leaves, chopped

1 bay leaf
1 medium onion, sliced
1/3 cup uncooked barley
2 carrots, sliced
1 cup shredded cabbage
1 medium tomato, peeled, diced
1 cup fresh green beans, cut in 1-inch pieces
1 turnip or parsnip, diced

Sort and soak beans; see How To Prepare Dried Beans, pages 5 and 6. While beans are soaking, prepare stock. In a 4-quart pot, combine beef shanks or soup bones, 9 cups water, bouillon cubes, salt, peppercorns, celery, bay leaf and onion. Bring to a boil; reduce heat. Cover and simmer 2 hours. Remove beef shanks or soup bones. Cut meat from bones and discard bones. Dice meat and set aside. Strain stock; discarding vegetables, peppercorns and bay leaf. Return stock to the pot. Drain beans; discard soak water. Add soaked beans and barley to stock. Bring to a boil. Reduce heat. Cover and simmer until beans are tender, about 1 hour. Add carrots, cabbage, tomato, green beans and turnip or parsnip. Add diced beef to soup. Simmer another 30 minutes. Makes 8 servings.

Seafood Bean Chowder

Cooked crab can be substituted for the shrimp.

2 tablespoons finely chopped onion
2 tablespoons butter or margarine
3 tablespoons all-purpose flour
1/4 teaspoon dry mustard
1 (10-3/4-oz.) can chicken broth
2 cups whole milk
1 (16-oz.) can cream-style corn

1 (10-oz.) pkg. frozen baby lima beans, thawed
1/4 teaspoon salt
1/8 teaspoon white pepper
1 cup cooked shrimp
4 tablespoons dry white wine, if desired
1 hard-cooked egg, sieved

In a large saucepan, sauté onion in butter or margarine until tender but not browned. Add flour and mustard, mixing well. Remove from heat. Slowly pour in chicken broth and milk, stirring constantly to prevent lumping. Continue to stir constantly over medium heat until mixture comes to a boil. Stir in corn, lima beans, salt, white pepper and shrimp. Cover and simmer 10 minutes, stirring frequently. If desired, stir in wine before serving. Garnish each serving with a sprinkle of sieved egg. Makes 6 to 8 servings.

Black-Eyed Pea Soup

To be sure you like the flavor, taste the sherry before adding it to the soup.

1 lb. dried black-eyed peas
3/4 cup chopped onion
2 tablespoons butter or margarine
1 (10-3/4-oz.) can chicken broth
6 cups water
1 bay leaf

1/4 teaspoon dried leaf thyme
2 teaspoons salt
1 (16-oz.) can tomatoes, undrained, diced
4 hot dogs, sliced
2 tablespoons dry sherry, if desired

Sort and rinse peas. In a 4-quart pot, sauté onions in butter or margarine until tender but not browned. Add rinsed peas, broth, water, bay leaf, thyme and salt. Bring to a boil; reduce heat. Cover and simmer until peas are tender, 1 to 1-1/2 hours. Add tomatoes. Stir in hot dog slices. Cover and simmer 30 minutes longer. If desired, add about 1 teaspoon sherry to each bowl before serving. Makes 6 to 8 servings.

Spanish Chicken Soup

Look for saffron, famous for flavoring Spanish paella, *in a gourmet shop.*

1 cup dried garbanzo beans or
  1 (15-oz.) can garbanzo beans
Water for soaking
1/2 (3-lb.) frying chicken
4 cups water
2 chicken bouillon cubes
1 (16-oz.) can tomatoes, undrained, diced
1/4 cup tomato paste

1 garlic clove, minced
1/2 cup chopped onion
1/3 cup chopped green pepper
2 tablespoons vegetable oil
1 (4-oz.) can diced or chopped green chilies
1 teaspoon salt
Pinch of saffron
1/2 to 1 cup garlic croutons, if desired

Sort and soak dried garbanzo beans; see How To Prepare Dried Beans, pages 5 and 6. Drain beans; discard soak water. If using canned garbanzo beans, drain and set aside. In a 4-quart pot, combine soaked dried beans, chicken, 4 cups water and bouillon cubes. Bring to a boil; reduce heat. Cover and simmer until chicken is tender, about 30 minutes. Remove chicken. Cut meat from bones and discard bones. Dice meat; set aside. If using dried beans, continue to simmer until tender, 30 to 45 minutes. If using canned beans, add to chicken stock without cooking. Add tomatoes, tomato paste and reserved chicken to cooked or canned bean mixture. Stir well. In a small skillet, sauté garlic, onion and green pepper in oil until onion is tender but not browned. Add sautéed mixture to soup. Stir in chilies, salt and saffron. Bring soup to a boil. Reduce heat and simmer 15 minutes. Ladle into soup bowls and sprinkle about 2 tablespoons croutons over each serving, if desired. Makes 4 to 6 servings.

Hungarian Bean Soup

You can find mild paprika in the supermarket and hot paprika in a gourmet shop.

2 cups dried pinto beans
Water for soaking
2 slices bacon
1/2 lb. pork cut in 1/2-inch cubes
3/4 cup chopped onion
1 garlic clove, minced
1 lb. beef or pork bones
1 (8-oz.) can tomato sauce

8 cups water
1/2 teaspoon dry mustard
1 tablespoon mild paprika
1-1/2 teaspoons salt
1 teaspoon Worcestershire sauce
2 teaspoons cider vinegar
1/4 teaspoon hot paprika, if desired
1/2 cup dairy sour cream, if desired

Sort and soak beans; see How To Prepare Dried Beans, pages 5 and 6. Drain beans; discard soak water. In a medium skillet, fry bacon until crisp. Drain on paper towels. Brown pork cubes in bacon drippings. Remove pork, set aside. Sauté onions and garlic in drippings until onion is tender but not browned. In a 4-quart pot, combine soaked beans, bones, browned pork, sautéed onion mixture, tomato sauce and 8 cups water. Mix well. Stir in mustard, mild paprika, salt, Worcestershire sauce, vinegar and hot paprika, if desired. Crumble cooked bacon over soup. Bring soup to a boil; reduce heat. Cover and simmer until beans and pork cubes are tender, about 1-1/2 hours. Remove bones. If desired, top each serving with a dollop of sour cream. Makes 8 servings.

Capitol Hill Special

It's similar to the soup made famous by hungry senators in Washington, D.C.

2 cups dried pea beans or small white beans
Water for soaking
7 cups water
1 (1-lb.) meaty smoked ham shank,
    cut in 3 or 4 pieces
1 garlic clove, minced

1/2 cup chopped onion
1 tablespoon bacon drippings or lard
1 teaspoon salt
1/2 teaspoon pepper
2 bay leaves

Sort and soak beans; see How To Prepare Dried Beans, pages 5 and 6. Drain beans; discard soak water. In a 4-quart pot, combine soaked beans, 7 cups water and ham shank pieces. In a small skillet, sauté garlic and onion in bacon drippings or lard until onion is tender but not browned. Add sautéed mixture to beans. Stir in salt, pepper and bay leaves. Bring beans to a boil; reduce heat. Cover and simmer until beans are tender, 1 to 1-1/2 hours. Remove ham shank pieces and bay leaves. Discard bay leaves. Cut meat from bones and discard bones. Dice meat. Remove about 2 cups of soup from pot and puree in blender or food processor. Add puree and diced ham to soup. Stir well. Heat 10 minutes longer before ladling into large soup bowls. Makes 4 to 6 servings.

Bean Medley

Popular pea beans are also known as navy beans.

1/2 cup dried pinto beans
1/2 cup dried pea beans or small white beans
Water for soaking
2 tablespoons vegetable oil
1/2 lb. beef shanks or meaty soup bones
1/2 cup chopped onion
1 carrot, sliced

7 cups water
4 beef bouillon cubes
1/4 teaspoon dry mustard
2 tablespoons chopped fresh parsley
1/4 cup dried green or yellow split peas
1/4 cup dried lentils
1/4 cup uncooked barley

Sort and soak beans; see How To Prepare Dried Beans, pages 5 and 6. Drain beans; discard soak water. Heat oil in a heavy 4-quart pot. Add beef shanks or soup bones; brown well. Move meat to one side and add onion and carrot. Sauté until onion is tender but not browned. Add soaked beans, 7 cups water, bouillon cubes, mustard and parsley. Bring to a boil; reduce heat. Cover and simmer 45 minutes. Sort and rinse peas and lentils. Add peas, lentils and barley to soup. Cover and simmer 30 to 45 minutes longer until both beans and peas are tender. Remove beef shanks or bones from soup. Cut meat from bones and discard bones. Dice meat and return to soup. Serve soup warm in soup mugs. Makes 4 to 6 servings.

Old-Country Lentil Soup

Hearty soup, crusty bread and a green salad add up to a complete meal.

4 slices bacon, diced
1 medium onion, chopped
2 medium carrots, sliced
1 large celery rib, sliced
1 lb. dried lentils
8 cups water

2 teaspoons salt
1/2 teaspoon pepper
1/2 teaspoon dried leaf thyme
2 bay leaves
1 large potato, peeled, diced
1 (1-lb.) ham shank, cut in 3 or 4 pieces

In a heavy 4-quart pot over medium heat, fry bacon until crisp. Drain on paper towels, reserving drippings in pot. Add onion, carrots and celery to drippings. Sauté until onion is tender but not browned. Sort and rinse lentils. Return bacon to pot. Add rinsed lentils, water, salt, pepper, thyme, bay leaves, potato and ham shank pieces. Bring to a boil; reduce heat. Cover and simmer until lentils are tender, about 45 minutes. Remove ham shank pieces and bay leaves. Discard bay leaves. Cut meat from bones and discard bones. Dice meat. Add diced meat to soup; stir gently. Serve generous helpings in soup bowls or mugs. Makes 4 to 6 servings.

Ginger Soup

You can easily shred fresh ginger with a hand grater.

2 cups dried Great Northern beans
Water for soaking
1 meaty soup bone
6 cups water
2 (10-1/2-oz.) cans beef broth
1 medium onion, sliced
1 tablespoon shredded peeled fresh ginger

2 tablespoons vegetable oil
1 teaspoon salt
1 tablespoon soy sauce
2 tablespoons cornstarch
1/4 cup water
1 medium green pepper
Chow Mein noodles, if desired

Sort and soak beans, see How To Prepare Dried Beans, pages 5 and 6. Drain beans; discard soak water. In a 4-quart pot, combine soaked beans, soup bone, 6 cups water and broth. In a medium skillet, sauté onion and shredded ginger in oil until onion is tender but not browned. Add to beans. Stir in salt and soy sauce. Bring to a boil; reduce heat. Cover and simmer until beans are tender, 1 to 1-1/2 hours. Mix cornstarch and 1/4 cup of water in a small bowl. Add to soup, stirring constantly. Bring soup to a boil. Cut green pepper lengthwise in 1/2-inch strips. Then cut in 2-inch pieces. Add green pepper pieces to soup; simmer 10 minutes. Sprinkle a few Chow Mein noodles over each serving, if desired. Makes 6 to 8 servings.

How To Shred Fresh Ginger
For Ginger Soup

1/Ginger's tough outer skin seals in the moisture. With a paring knife, cut the bark-like skin from fresh ginger.

2/Using a shredder or grater with small holes, shred the peeled ginger. If you have several hole sizes on your grater, use the side with the smallest holes.

Soybean Puree With Vegetables

Fill a cloth-lined bread basket with warmed pita bread to go with this nutritious soup.

1 cup dried soybeans	1 cup chopped celery
Water for soaking	1 cup chopped carrots
1 (1-inch) cube salt pork, sliced	2 tablespoons butter or margarine
1/2 cup chopped onion	1 cup canned tomatoes, undrained
4 cups water	1-1/2 teaspoons salt
1 garlic clove, minced	1 (10-3/4-oz.) can chicken broth
1 bay leaf	

Sort and soak soybeans; see How To Prepare Dried Beans, pages 5 and 6. Drain beans; discard soak water. In a small skillet, fry salt pork with onion until onion is tender but not browned. In a large saucepan, combine soaked soybeans, sautéed onion, salt pork, 4 cups water, garlic and bay leaf. Bring to a boil; reduce heat. Cover and simmer until beans are tender, about 3 hours. If necessary, add water during cooking to keep soybeans covered. Remove and discard bay leaf. Drain soybeans, reserving cooking liquid. Measure reserved cooking liquid and add water if necessary to make 2 cups. Puree soybeans in blender adding reserved cooking liquid as needed; set aside remaining liquid. In a medium skillet, sauté celery and carrots in butter or margarine. Add tomatoes, stirring to break up. Cover and cook over low heat 10 minutes. In a large saucepan, combine pureed beans, sautéed vegetables, salt, broth and remaining reserved cooking liquid. Cover and simmer 15 minutes, stirring frequently to prevent scorching. Makes 4 to 6 servings.

Mixed Bean Chowder

Chowder becomes a substantial meal when you add beans.

3/4 cup dried Great Northern beans	1 garlic clove, minced
3/4 cup dried pink beans or pinto beans	2 tablespoons butter or margarine
Water for soaking	1 medium potato, peeled, diced
4-1/2 cups water	1/2 cup diced green pepper
1-1/2 teaspoons salt	1/2 to 1 cup whole milk
3/4 cup chopped onion	

Sort and soak beans; see How To Prepare Dried Beans, pages 5 and 6. Drain beans; discard soak water. In a 4-quart pot, combine soaked beans, 4-1/2 cups water and salt. In a small skillet, sauté onion and garlic in butter or margarine until onion is tender but not browned. Add to beans. Bring to a boil; reduce heat. Cover and simmer until beans are almost tender, 1 hour. Add potato; simmer another 30 minutes. Remove 1 cup of bean-potato mixture. Mash in a small bowl with a potato masher or fork. Return mashed mixture to soup and stir well. Add green pepper and enough milk for desired consistency. Cook over low heat 10 minutes, stirring occasionally to prevent scorching. Makes 4 to 6 servings.

Brazilian Bean Soup

For orange sections without tough membranes, cut on both sides of the membrane.

1 lb. dried black beans
Water for soaking
1 (10-1/2-oz.) can beef broth
6 cups water
4 oz. pepperoni, thinly sliced
1/2 teaspoon salt

3 slices bacon
1 medium onion, sliced
3/4 cup red wine
2 medium oranges
Orange peel twists, if desired

Sort and soak beans, see How To Prepare Dried Beans, pages 5 and 6. Drain beans; discard soak water. In a heavy 4-quart pot, combine soaked beans, beef broth, 6 cups water, pepperoni and salt. In a medium skillet, fry bacon until crisp. Drain on paper towels. Crumble; set aside. Sauté onion in bacon drippings until onion is tender but not browned. Add sautéed onion to beans. Bring bean mixture to a boil; reduce heat. Cover and simmer until beans are tender, 1 to 1-1/2 hours. Stir in red wine. Simmer 30 minutes longer. Remove 1 cup of beans with a slotted spoon. In a small bowl, mash removed beans with a potato masher or fork. Return mashed beans to soup. Peel and section oranges. Stir orange sections into soup. Heat 5 minutes. Ladle soup into bowls and garnish with a twist of orange peel, if desired. Makes 6 to 8 servings.

Black Bean Soup

The ham hock adds flavor. Reserve the cooked meat for salads and casseroles.

1 lb. dried black beans
Water for soaking
1/2 cup chopped onion
1 garlic clove, minced
1/2 cup chopped celery
2 tablespoons butter or margarine
1 (3/4-lb.) meaty smoked ham hock
1/2 lemon

4 whole cloves
1 (10-1/2-oz.) can beef broth
6 cups water
1 bay leaf
Pinch of ground thyme
1/4 cup dry sherry
2 hard-cooked eggs, sieved
Chopped green onion

Sort and soak beans; see How To Prepare Dried Beans, pages 5 and 6. Drain beans; discard soak water. In a small skillet, sauté onion, garlic and celery in butter or margarine until onion is tender but not browned. In a 4-quart pot, combine soaked beans, sautéed vegetables and ham hock. Cut lemon half into quarters and stick a clove into each quarter. Add lemon quarters, broth, 6 cups water, bay leaf and thyme to beans; stir well. Bring to a boil; reduce heat. Cover and simmer until beans are very tender, 1 to 1-1/2 hours. Remove ham hock and bay leaf. Reserve ham hock for another use; discard bay leaf. Puree soup in blender or food mill. For a smoother soup, put through a sieve to remove bean coats. Return soup to pot. Stir in sherry. Garnish each serving with sieved egg and chopped green onion. Makes 4 to 6 servings.

Chick Pea & Sausage Soup

Whether you call them chick peas, garbanzos *or* ceci beans, *they add delightful crunch.*

2 cups dried garbanzo beans
Water for soaking
6 cups water
3 chicken bouillon cubes
1 bay leaf
10 peppercorns
1/2 lb. sweet or hot Italian sausage,
   cut in 1-inch pieces

1/2 cup chopped onion
1/2 cup chopped green pepper
1 garlic clove, minced
1/2 teaspoon Worcestershire sauce
1/2 teaspoon paprika
1 medium potato, peeled, diced
1/2 teaspoon salt
Seasoned croutons, if desired

Sort and soak beans; see How To Prepare Dried Beans, pages 5 and 6. Drain beans; discard soak water. In a 4-quart pot, combine soaked beans, 6 cups water, bouillon cubes, bay leaf and peppercorns. Bring to a boil; reduce heat. Cover and simmer until beans are tender, 1 to 1-1/2 hours. Remove and discard bay leaf and peppercorns. In a medium skillet, fry sausage until some fat is rendered. Add onions, green pepper and garlic. Sauté until onion is softened. Add sausage-onion mixture to cooked beans. Stir in Worcestershire sauce, paprika, potato and salt. Cover and simmer 30 minutes longer or until potato is tender. Ladle into soup mugs and top with seasoned croutons, if desired. Makes 4 to 6 servings.

Variation

Use 2 (15-ounce) cans garbanzo beans in place of 2 cups dried garbanzo beans. Do not soak or cook canned beans. Reduce water to 3 cups. Drain beans. Combine with water, bouillon cubes, bay leaf, peppercorns, cooked sausage-onion mixture, Worcestershire sauce, paprika, potato and salt. Cook and serve as directed.

Squaw Bean Soup

Mashing cooked beans and stirring them back into the soup makes a thicker soup.

2 cups dried pea beans or small white beans
Water for soaking
8 cups water
4 slices bacon, diced
1 cup chopped onion
1 garlic clove, minced
1/2 cup chopped celery

2 teaspoons salt
1/8 teaspoon pepper
1/2 teaspoon dried leaf basil
1/4 teaspoon dried leaf oregano
1 lb. winter squash such as Hubbard,
   banana or acorn

Sort and soak beans; see How To Prepare Dried Beans, pages 5 and 6. Drain beans; discard soak water. In a 4-quart pot, combine soaked beans and 8 cups water. In a medium skillet, fry bacon until crisp. Drain on paper towels. Pour all but 2 tablespoons bacon drippings from skillet. Sauté onion, garlic and celery in drippings until onion is tender but not browned. Add sautéed vegetables to beans. Stir in salt, pepper, basil and oregano. Bring to a boil; reduce heat. Cover and simmer 1 hour. Peel and cut squash into 1-inch cubes. Add squash to beans. Cook 30 minutes longer. Remove 1 cup of beans from soup. Mash beans in a small bowl with a fork and stir into soup to thicken. Simmer 10 minutes, stirring occasionally. Makes 6 to 8 servings.

Old-Fashioned Split Pea Soup

Enjoy this traditional soup with your favorite cornbread.

1 lb. green split peas
1 cup chopped celery
1 cup chopped onion
1 garlic clove, minced
2 tablespoons vegetable oil
1 (1-lb.) meaty ham shank, cut in 3 or 4 pieces

1 medium potato, peeled, diced
1/4 teaspoon pepper
8 cups water
2 chicken bouillon cubes
1 bay leaf
1/2 cup whole milk

Sort and rinse peas. In a heavy 4-quart pot, sauté celery, onion and garlic in oil until onion is tender but not browned. Add rinsed peas, ham shank pieces, potato, pepper, water, bouillon cubes and bay leaf. Bring to a boil; reduce heat. Cover and simmer until peas are very tender, about 45 minutes. Remove and discard bay leaf. Remove ham shank pieces. Cut meat from bones and discard bones. Dice meat; set aside. Puree soup in blender or food processor and return to pot. Stir in diced meat and milk. Cook over medium heat 10 minutes, stirring frequently. Serve steaming hot in large soup bowls. Makes 6 to 8 servings.

Split Pea Soup With Mushrooms

Sauté means to stir gently in hot butter or margarine over medium heat.

1 lb. dried yellow split peas
8 cups water
3 chicken bouillon cubes
1 tomato, peeled, chopped
3/4 cup sliced carrot
3/4 cup chopped celery
1/2 cup chopped onion

8 oz. fresh mushrooms, sliced
2 tablespoons butter or margarine
2 tablespoons chopped fresh parsley
1 bay leaf
1/2 teaspoon salt
1/2 teaspoon dried leaf marjoram
2 tablespoons butter or margarine

Sort and rinse peas. In a 4-quart pot, combine rinsed peas, water, bouillon cubes and tomato. In a medium skillet, sauté carrot, celery, onion and 1 cup mushrooms in 2 tablespoons butter or margarine until onion is tender but not browned. Add vegetable mixture to peas. Stir parsley, bay leaf, salt and marjoram into peas. Bring to a boil; reduce heat. Cover and simmer until peas are tender, about 45 minutes. In a small skillet, sauté remaining mushrooms in 2 tablespoons butter or margarine 5 minutes. Add to peas and vegetable mixture. Simmer 10 minutes longer. Makes 6 to 8 servings.

Bean cooking liquid is a flavorful substitute for broth or stock in your favorite recipes.

Leafy Spinach & Bean Soup

This light soup is excellent with a sandwich for Sunday's supper.

1 cup dried Great Northern beans
Water for soaking
2-1/2 cups water
3/4 teaspoon salt
1/4 teaspoon pepper
1 bay leaf

1/2 cup finely chopped onion
1 garlic clove, minced
2 tablespoons butter or margarine
3 cups chicken broth
2 cups torn fresh spinach leaves
Freshly grated Parmesan cheese

Sort and soak beans; see How To Prepare Dried Beans, pages 5 and 6. Drain beans; discard soak water. In a medium saucepan, combine soaked beans, 2-1/2 cups water, salt, pepper and bay leaf Bring to a boil; reduce heat. Cover and simmer until beans are tender, 1 to 1-1/2 hours. In a small skillet, sauté onion and garlic in butter or margarine until onion is tender but not browned. Add sautéed onion mixture and chicken broth to beans. Cover and simmer 10 minutes longer. Add spinach to soup. Cook 5 minutes. Remove and discard bay leaf. Ladle soup into soup bowls and sprinkle with Parmesan cheese. Makes 4 servings.

Mama's Homemade Chili

For a milder chili, use a little less cayenne pepper.

3 cups drained, cooked red kidney beans,
    page 15, or 2 (15-oz.) cans red kidney beans,
    drained
1 lb. ground beef
1 cup chopped onion
1 cup chopped celery
2 garlic cloves, minced

1 (28-oz.) can tomatoes, undrained, diced
1 (12-oz.) can tomato juice
1 (10-1/2-oz.) can beef broth
1 to 2 tablespoons chili powder
2 teaspoons salt
1/8 teaspoon cayenne pepper

Prepare beans. Brown beef in a large skillet until no longer pink. Drain all but about 2 tablespoons drippings from skillet. Push beef to one side of skillet. Sauté onion, celery and garlic in skillet until onion is tender but not browned. Stir beef into onion mixture. In a 4-quart pot, combine beef mixture, tomatoes, tomato juice, beef broth, chili powder, salt, cayenne pepper and beans. Bring to a boil; reduce heat. Cover and simmer 45 minutes. Serve piping hot. Makes 6 to 8 servings.

One 10 3/4-ounce can of chicken or beef broth equals 1-1/4 cups broth.

Lima Bean Soup

If you like thick soup, cook another diced, peeled potato with the lima beans.

1 (10-oz.) pkg. frozen baby lima beans
1 medium potato, peeled, diced
1 (10-3/4-oz.) can chicken broth
1 cup water
1/2 cup chopped green pepper
1/2 cup chopped onion
1 garlic clove, minced

1 tablespoon butter or margarine
2 tablespoons chopped fresh parsley
1/4 teaspoon dried leaf thyme
1/4 teaspoon dried leaf basil
1/2 teaspoon salt
1 cup cottage cheese
1/2 cup whole milk

In a large saucepan, combine lima beans, potato, chicken broth and water. In a small skillet, sauté green pepper, onion and garlic in butter or margarine until onion is tender but not browned. Add sautéed mixture to lima beans. Stir in parsley, thyme, basil and salt. Bring to a boil; reduce heat. Cover and simmer 30 minutes. Stir in cottage cheese and milk. Heat 10 minutes longer, stirring occasionally, until cheese begins to melt. Serve immediately. Makes 4 servings.

Lentil Soup & Dumplings

If you don't have a food processor, use a hand grater to shred cheese and meat.

1 cup dried lentils
4 cups water
1/2 teaspoon salt
2 chicken bouillon cubes
1 cup sliced carrot

1 cup sliced celery
1 medium onion, sliced
2 tablespoons vegetable oil
1-1/2 cups whole milk
Ham & Cheese Dumplings, see below

Ham & Cheese Dumplings:
6 tablespoons butter or margarine
3/4 cup shredded Swiss cheese
1/4 cup shredded ham or luncheon meat

1/4 cup all-purpose flour
1 egg
1/2 teaspoon dry mustard

Sort and rinse lentils. In a 4-quart pot, combine rinsed lentils, water, salt and bouillon cubes. Bring to a boil. Cook 2 minutes, stirring occasionally. Remove from heat. In a medium skillet, sauté carrot, celery and onion in oil until onion is tender but not browned. Stir sautéed vegetables into lentils. Bring to a boil; reduce heat. Cover and simmer until lentils are tender, about 45 minutes. Stir in milk. Continue cooking until soup is hot but not boiling. Prepare dumplings. Drop dumplings into hot soup. Cover and simmer until dumplings are cooked, about 15 minutes. Ladle soup and 3 or 4 dumplings into each soup bowl. Makes 6 to 8 servings.

Ham & Cheese Dumplings:
In a small bowl, cream together butter or margarine, cheese, ham or luncheon meat and flour. Stir in egg and mustard. Dust hands with flour and shape rounded teaspoons of dumpling mixture into small balls. Makes about 24 dumplings.

Corn-Bean Chowder

Ask your butcher to cut the ham shank into 3 or 4 pieces.

2 cups dried Great Northern beans
Water for soaking
5 cups water
1 (1-lb.) meaty ham shank, cut in 3 or 4 pieces
1/2 cup chopped onion

1 teaspoon salt
1/2 cup chopped green pepper
1 tablespoon butter or margarine
1 (16-oz.) can whole-kernel corn, drained
1 to 1-1/2 cups whole milk

Sort and soak beans; see How To Prepare Dried Beans, pages 5 and 6. Drain beans; discard soak water. In a 4-quart pot, combine soaked beans, 5 cups water, ham shank pieces, onion and salt. Bring to a boil; reduce heat. Cover and simmer until beans are tender, 1 to 1-1/2 hours. Remove ham shank pieces. Cut meat from bones and discard bones. Dice meat and set aside. Mash beans slightly with a potato masher. In a small skillet, sauté green pepper in butter or margarine. Add sautéed green pepper, diced ham, corn and milk to beans. Heat over low heat, stirring frequently. Do not boil. Serve immediately. Makes 6 to 8 servings.

How To Make
Lentil Soup & Dumplings

1/Drop walnut-size dumplings into simmering soup. Cover and simmer about 15 minutes. Do not boil or stir vigorously. Too much agitation will cause dumplings to fall apart.

2/Dumplings will expand during cooking and become very tender. Be gentle when you ladle them into the soup bowls.

Frijole Cheese Soup

Frijole (free-hoe-lay) is Spanish for bean. *Serve this soup with warm buttered flour tortillas.*

2 cups dried pinto beans
Water for soaking
5 cups water
1 (1-inch) cube salt pork or 2 slices bacon,
   cut in half
1/2 cup chopped onion
1-1/2 teaspoons salt

1 (16-oz.) can tomatoes, undrained, diced
2 teaspoons chili powder
1/2 teaspoon ground cumin
1/4 teaspoon dried leaf oregano
1 to 2 cups water
1-1/2 cups shredded Cheddar cheese

Sort and soak beans; see How To Prepare Dried Beans, pages 5 and 6. Drain beans; discard soak water. In a large saucepan, combine soaked beans, 5 cups water, salt pork or bacon, onion and salt. Bring to a boil; reduce heat. Cover and simmer until beans are tender, 1 to 1-1/2 hours. Remove and discard salt pork or bacon. Drain beans, reserving liquid. Puree beans 1 or 2 cups at a time in blender, using reserved cooking liquid as needed. In a 4-quart pot, combine pureed beans, remaining reserved cooking liquid, tomatoes, chili powder, cumin, oregano and 1 cup water. Add more water for a thinner consistency. Cover and simmer 20 minutes. Add cheese. Stir constantly over medium heat until cheese melts. Serve immediately. Makes 4 to 6 servings.

Variation

Substitute 1 small ham hock for salt pork or bacon.

Bean With Bacon Soup

Homemade is always better!

2 cups dried pea beans
Water for soaking
6 cups water
2 teaspoons salt
1 bay leaf

6 slices bacon
1 cup chopped onions
2/3 cup diced carrots
1/4 cup chopped celery leaves
1/2 to 1 cup tomato juice

Sort and soak beans; see How To Prepare Dried Beans, pages 5 and 6. Drain beans; discard soak water. In a large saucepan, combine soaked beans, 6 cups water, salt and bay leaf. In a small skillet, fry bacon until crisp. Drain on paper towels. Crumble bacon. Pour all but 2 tablespoons bacon drippings from skillet. Sauté onions, carrots and celery leaves in bacon drippings until onion is tender but not browned. Stir sautéed vegetables into beans. Bring to a boil; reduce heat. Cover and simmer until beans are tender, 1 to 1-1/2 hours. Remove and discard bay leaf. Remove 1 cup of beans and set aside. Drain remaining beans, reserving cooking liquid. Add water to cooking liquid if necessary to measure 2 cups. Combine beans and 2 cups reserved cooking liquid in blender or food processor; puree. Return puree and 1 cup reserved beans to saucepan. Stir in 1/2 cup tomato juice. Add more if a thinner consistency is desired. Heat 10 minutes until thoroughly warmed. Makes 4 to 6 servings.

Garden Vegetable Soup

The increased surface area of julienne vegetables lets more flavor escape and blend into the broth.

1 celery rib including leaves
1 carrot
1/4 cup butter or margarine
1/2 cup chopped green onions
8 medium fresh mushrooms, thinly sliced
2 (10-3/4-oz.) cans chicken broth
2-1/2 cups water

2 chicken bouillon cubes
1/2 teaspoon salt
1/8 teaspoon pepper
1/2 teaspoon dried leaf basil
1/2 lb. fresh green beans, cut in diagonal
   1/2-inch slices
2 cups torn fresh spinach leaves

Cut celery and carrot into julienne, or matchstick, pieces. In a 4-quart heavy pot, melt butter or margarine over medium heat. Sauté green onions, mushrooms and julienned celery and carrot until onion is tender but not browned. Stir in chicken broth, water, bouillon cubes, salt, pepper and basil. Bring to a boil; reduce heat. Cover and simmer 10 minutes. Add green beans. Simmer 15 minutes longer. Stir in spinach. Simmer 3 minutes. Serve immediately. Makes 6 to 8 servings.

Lentil Tomato Soup

When onion is sautéed until it's tender but not browned, it is sometimes called translucent.

1-1/2 cups dried lentils
5 cups water
1/2 cup chopped onion
1 garlic clove, minced
1 tablespoon butter or margarine
2 teaspoons salt
1/8 teaspoon pepper

2 teaspoons sugar
1/4 teaspoon dried leaf oregano
1/4 teaspoon dried leaf basil
1 tablespoon chopped fresh parsley
1 (16-oz.) can tomatoes, undrained, diced
3 tablespoons tomato paste
Additional fresh parsley, if desired

Sort and rinse lentils. In a large saucepan, combine rinsed lentils and water. In a small skillet, sauté onion and garlic in butter or margarine until onion is tender but not browned. Add to lentils. Stir in salt, pepper, sugar, oregano, basil and parsley. Bring to a boil; reduce heat. Cover and simmer until lentils are tender, about 45 minutes. Add tomatoes and tomato paste. Stir well. Simmer 15 minutes longer. Garnish each bowl with a parsley sprig, if desired. Makes 4 servings.

Store fresh ginger in the refrigerator in a plastic bag up to 2 weeks. For longer storage—up to 1 year—peel and slice the ginger. Cover it with dry sherry and store it in the refrigerator.

Salads

To many of us, salad means a bowl of lettuce with a sliced tomato. But by using a variety of fruits and vegetables, including fresh-cooked or leftover beans, salad possibilities are endless. Spring Garden Salad combines green beans, peas, asparagus, cucumber and radishes. Eggplant Salad uses red kidney beans, Great Northern beans, green pepper, eggplant and tomato for a deliciously different taste. Adding a cup of cooked garbanzo beans or red kidney beans to the usual tossed salad makes it more interesting and fresh mung bean sprouts can give a special crunch. Substitute Beans In Aspic on the buffet table for tomato aspic and wait for the compliments. Serve Apple-Bean Slaw or Sprout Slaw with sandwiches instead of ordinary cole slaw and watch it disappear!

The best salads are made with fresh vegetables and fruits. Unfortunately, we can enjoy fresh salads only at certain times of the year. Substituting cooked frozen vegetables for cooked fresh vegetables in salads will help bring summer spirit to your winter meals. Canned vegetables can be used in place of fresh vegetables but they are best in canned bean salads such as Bean Bonanza or Sauerkraut Marinade.

Salad dressings begin on page 67.

Salad Buffet
Picnic Salad, page 60
Sunshine Salad, page 53
Beans In Aspic, page 65
Watermelon Boat Fruit Salad
Tea Sandwiches
Coffee Mousse

Italian Dinner
Antipasto Platter, page 138
Breadsticks
Veal Parmigiana
Poppy Seed Noodles
Thick Tomato Slices Piled With
Eggplant Salad, page 66
Fresh Strawberry Ice

Sunshine Salad

Delicious with either dressing, but more colorful with Sweet & Sour Honey Dressing.

2 cups drained cooked Great Northern beans,
    page 15, or 1 (15-oz.) can cannellini beans,
    drained
1/3 to 1/2 cup Sweet & Sour Honey Dressing,
    page 71, or Yogurt Mayonnaise, page 70
2 cups diced cooked chicken

1 (12-oz.) can whole-kernel corn, drained
1 (4-oz.) jar button mushrooms, drained
1 medium avocado, peeled, diced
1 (16-oz.) can peach slices, drained
4 green onions, sliced
2 tablespoons chopped fresh parsley

Prepare beans and Sweet and Sour Honey Dressing or Yogurt Mayonnaise. In a medium bowl, combine beans, chicken, corn, mushrooms, avocado, peach slices, green onions and parsley. Stir gently. Pour dressing over salad and fold to mix. Refrigerate until ready to serve. Makes 6 to 8 servings.

Orange-Bean Salad

This slightly sweet salad goes well with roast meats—especially pork.

2 cups drained cooked red kidney beans,
    page 15, or 1 (15-oz.) can red kidney
    beans, drained
1/4 to 1/3 cup Sweet & Sour Honey Dressing,
    page 71
1 (11-oz.) can mandarin orange sections,
    drained

1 (16-oz.) can cut green beans, drained
1/2 cup chopped red onion
1/4 cup chopped fresh parsley
1 (3-oz.) can French-fried onions

Prepare kidney beans and Sweet & Sour Honey Dressing. In a salad bowl, combine kidney beans, orange sections, green beans, onion and parsley. Toss gently. Pour dressing over salad; toss again. Refrigerate until ready to serve. Garnish with French-fried onions. Makes 6 to 8 servings.

Apple-Bean Slaw

Unpeeled apple adds color to this pale green and yellow salad.

2 cups drained cooked large lima beans,
    page 15
1/2 to 3/4 cup Yogurt Mayonnaise, page 70

3 cups shredded cabbage
1 large red apple, unpeeled, cored, diced
2 oz. Swiss cheese, cubed

Prepare lima beans and Yogurt Mayonnaise. Combine lima beans, cabbage, apple and cheese in a salad bowl. Mix well. Pour dressing over salad. Stir to coat all ingredients. Refrigerate until ready to serve. Makes 6 to 8 servings.

Polynesian Boats

If you can't find a fresh pineapple, use the variation below.

1 fresh pineapple
1 (11-oz.) can mandarin oranges
1-1/2 cups mung bean sprouts
1 cup diced cooked chicken
1 green onion, sliced
1/3 cup canned sliced water chestnuts

1/3 cup dairy sour cream
3 tablespoons mayonnaise
1 tablespoon orange-flavored liqueur
   such as curaçao or Grand Marnier
1/2 cup coarsely chopped macadamia nuts,
   almonds or pistachios

To prepare boats, stand a large pineapple on end. Cut pineapple in half lengthwise with a long sharp knife, cutting through the leaves. Cut each half in half again to make 4 boats. Remove the pineapple fruit from the shell with a long paring knife, leaving a 1/2-inch thick shell. Remove the core and eyes from the pineapple fruit. Dice enough pineapple fruit to measure 1 cup. Thoroughly drain diced pineapple and orange sections in a sieve, reserving liquid for another use. Wash and drain bean sprouts in a colander. In a medium bowl, combine drained fruit, bean sprouts, chicken, green onion and water chestnuts. Toss lightly. In a small bowl, stir sour cream, mayonnaise and orange liqueur. Carefully fold dressing and nuts into salad. Serve in pineapple boats. Makes 4 servings.

Variation

Substitute 1 (8-ounce) can of crushed pineapple for 1 cup of fresh pineapple. Serve in lettuce cups.

Pineapple-Pinto Plates

Who would think a bean salad could be so elegant!

2 cups drained cooked pinto beans, page 15,
   or 1 (15-oz.) can pinto beans, drained
1/4 cup Sesame Seed Dressing, page 73
1/2 cup diced green pepper
2 green onions, chopped
1/2 teaspoon dried dill weed

1/2 teaspoon salt
1/8 teaspoon black pepper
1 (8-oz.) can pineapple rings or slices, drained
Red leaf lettuce
4 sprigs fresh parsley

Prepare pinto beans and Sesame Seed Dressing. In a medium bowl, combine beans, green pepper, green onions, dill weed, salt and black pepper. Stir well. Reserve 2 pineapple rings; cover and refrigerate. Chop remaining pineapple rings and add to bean mixture. Pour dressing over salad. Stir well. Refrigerate until ready to serve. Arrange lettuce leaves on 4 salad plates. Mound salad on lettuce leaves. Cut reserved pineapple rings in half. Twist and place on top of each salad. Garnish with a sprig of parsley. Makes 4 servings.

Sprout Slaw

Not an ordinary slaw, this sprout slaw is deliciously different.

3/4 cup Yogurt Mayonnaise, page 70
2 cups mung bean sprouts

1 cup grated carrot
1 cup diced celery

Prepare Yogurt Mayonnaise. Wash and drain bean sprouts in a colander. Combine bean sprouts, carrot and celery in a salad bowl. Pour dressing over salad. Stir until all ingredients are coated. Refrigerate until ready to serve. Makes 4 servings.

Spinach & Sprouts

Light and refreshing.

1/4 to 1/3 cup Sweet & Sour Honey Dressing,
 page 71
4 cups fresh spinach leaves

2 cups mung bean sprouts or lentil sprouts
2 slices bacon

Prepare Sweet & Sour Honey Dressing. Wash and dry spinach leaves. Tear into bite-size pieces into a salad bowl. Wash and drain sprouts in a colander. Add to spinach. In a small skillet, fry bacon until crisp. Drain on a paper towel. Crumble bacon over spinach. Pour dressing over salad; toss lightly. Serve immediately or refrigerate briefly until ready to serve. Makes 4 to 6 servings.

Creamy Vegetable Toss

Remove vegetables from the heat as soon as they are crisp-tender—don't overcook!

1 cup water
1 teaspoon salt
3/4 lb. fresh green beans,
 cut in 2-inch pieces
1/2 lb. fresh broccoli, cut in bite-size flowerets

1 (6-oz.) jar marinated artichoke hearts,
 drained, cut in quarters
4 green onions, chopped
1/4 to 1/3 cup buttermilk-style salad dressing

Using 2 medium saucepans, bring 1/2 cup water and 1/2 teaspoon salt to boil in each saucepan. Cook beans in one saucepan and broccoli in the other saucepan until both vegetables are crisp-tender. Drain vegetables well. Combine cooked grean beans and broccoli, artichoke hearts, green onions and salad dressing. Mix gently. Refrigerate 6 hours or overnight. Makes 4 servings.

Variation

If fresh vegetables aren't available, use 1 (10-ounce) package cut green beans and 1 (10-ounce) package frozen chopped broccoli. Cook vegetables according to package directions, drain and combine with artichoke hearts, green onions and salad dressing. Refrigerate as directed.

Bean Bonanza

Prepare this take-off on three-bean salad at least 24 hours before serving.

1 (16-oz.) can cut green beans, drained
1 (16-oz.) can baby lima beans, drained
1 (15-oz.) can red kidney beans, drained
1 (15-oz.) can garbanzo beans, drained
2 celery ribs, thinly sliced
1 cup diced green pepper
1/2 cup chopped onion
1/3 cup chopped pimiento

1/2 cup vegetable oil
1/2 cup vinegar
3/4 cup sugar
1 teaspoon salt
1/2 teaspoon garlic salt
1/2 teaspoon black pepper
1 teaspoon celery salt

In a large bowl, combine all drained beans, celery, green pepper, onion and pimiento. In a small bowl or container with a tight-fitting lid, combine oil, vinegar, sugar, salt, garlic salt, black pepper and celery salt. Shake vigorously about 1 minute. Pour over bean mixture; stir. Cover and refrigerate at least 24 hours before serving. Makes 10 to 12 servings.

Hong Kong Garden Salad

For those who complain about the lack of a fresh salad with their Chinese dinner.

1/4 cup Mustard French Dressing, page 69
2 cups mung bean sprouts
1 cucumber, peeled, thinly sliced

1 avocado, peeled, diced
2 tablespoons chopped canned pimiento
1 tablespoon chopped chives

Prepare Mustard French Dressing. Wash and drain bean sprouts in a colander. Combine sprouts, cucumber, avocado, pimiento and chives in a salad bowl; toss to mix. Pour dressing over salad; toss again. Refrigerate until ready to serve but serve within 1 hour. Makes 4 servings.

Salami & Rice Salad

Make lettuce cups from the stiff inner lettuce leaves which are slightly rounded.

2 cups drained cooked red beans, page 15,
  or 1 (15-oz.) can red kidney beans, drained
1/3 to 1/2 cup Mustard French Dressing,
  page 69
2 cups water
1 teaspoon salt

1 cup uncooked rice
2/3 cup chopped red onion
1 cup diced salami
1/3 cup diced green pepper
4 to 6 lettuce cups

Prepare beans and Mustard French Dressing. In a medium saucepan, bring water and salt to a boil. Add rice; reduce heat to lowest setting. Cover and simmer 20 minutes. In a medium bowl, combine cooked rice, beans, onion, salami and green pepper. Stir well. Pour dressing over salad; stir. Refrigerate 2 hours before serving. Spoon into lettuce cups. Makes 4 to 6 servings.

Lemony Limas

Make it in the morning and it goes from refrigerator to table for dinner.

1/2 cup water
1/2 teaspoon salt
1 (10-oz.) pkg. frozen baby lima beans
1/2 cup shredded carrot
1/4 cup chopped green onions

2 tablespoons chopped fresh parsley
2 tablespoons lemon juice
1/4 cup vegetable oil
1/8 teaspoon pepper
1 garlic clove, minced

Bring water and salt to a boil in a small saucepan. Add lima beans; bring to a boil again. Reduce heat. Cover and simmer 10 minutes. Drain. In a medium bowl, combine cooked lima beans, carrot, green onions and parsley; mix well. In a small container with a tight-fitting lid, combine lemon juice, oil, pepper and garlic. Shake vigorously about 1 minute. Pour dressing over salad; stir gently. Refrigerate 6 hours or overnight. Makes 4 servings.

Shrimp & Marinated Vegetables

A treat in the fall when fresh brussels sprouts and cauliflower are available.

1 cup drained cooked garbanzo beans,
    page 15, or 1 (8-oz.) can garbanzo beans,
    drained
1/2 cup Tangy Lemon Dressing, page 71
1/2 cup water
1/4 teaspoon salt
1/2 lb. fresh brussels sprouts, trimmed
1/2 lb. fresh broccoli, cut in small spears
1/2 small cauliflower
1/2 cup water

1/4 teaspoon salt
1 (10-oz.) pkg. frozen cut green beans,
    cooked, drained
1/2 cup sliced ripe olives
2 cups water
1/2 teaspoon salt
8 oz. fresh or frozen small shrimp,
    peeled, deveined
Lettuce leaves

Prepare garbanzo beans and Tangy Lemon Dressing. In a medium saucepan, bring 1/2 cup water and 1/4 teaspoon salt to a boil. Add brussels sprouts and broccoli spears. Bring water to a boil again; reduce heat. Cover and simmer 8 minutes. Add more water during cooking if necessary. Quickly drain cooked vegetables and plunge into cold water. Wash cauliflower. Remove leaves and stalk; break into flowerets. In a medium saucepan, bring 1/2 cup water and 1/4 teaspoon salt to a boil. Add cauliflower. Bring water to a boil again; reduce heat. Simmer uncovered 5 minutes. Quickly drain cauliflower and plunge into cold water. In a large bowl, combine cooked brussels sprouts, broccoli, cauliflower and green beans. Add olives and garbanzo beans; toss lightly. Pour Tangy Lemon Dressing over salad; toss lightly. Refrigerate 6 to 8 hours or overnight. An hour before serving, prepare shrimp. In a medium saucepan, bring 2 cups water and 1/2 teaspoon salt to a boil. Add shrimp. Bring water to a boil again. Boil 3 minutes; if using frozen precooked shrimp, let boil only 1 minute. Drain and cool in ice-cold water. Fold chilled cooked shrimp into salad. Refrigerate until serving time. Arrange on lettuce leaves. Makes 6 servings.

Sauerkraut Marinade

Prepare this tasty salad the day before you want to serve it.

1 cup drained cooked garbanzo beans,
   page 15, or 1/2 (15-oz.) can garbanzo
   beans, drained
1 cup drained cooked red kidney beans,
   page 15, or 1 (8-oz.) can red kidney
   beans, drained
1 (16-oz.) can sauerkraut, drained

1/2 cup chopped celery
1/3 cup diced green pepper
1 tablespoon chopped pimiento
1/2 cup sugar
1/3 cup vegetable oil
1/3 cup vinegar

Prepare garbanzo beans and red kidney beans. In a medium bowl, combine sauerkraut, garbanzo beans, red kidney beans, celery, green pepper and pimiento. To make marinade, stir sugar, oil and vinegar in a small bowl. Pour marinade over salad; mix well. Refrigerate several hours or overnight. Makes 6 to 8 servings.

How To Make
Shrimp & Marinated Vegetables

1/With a paring knife, cut base and outer leaves from washed brussels sprouts. Do not cut above point where the leaves are attached or the sprouts will fall apart while cooking.

2/Wash and trim half a fresh cauliflower. With your fingers break the cauliflower half into flowerets.

Shrimp & Bean Cocktail

An attractive appetizer or salad—and less expensive than shrimp cocktail!

2 cups drained cooked Great Northern beans,
    page 15, or 1 (15-oz.) can cannellini
    beans, drained
2 tablespoons vegetable oil
1 teaspoon dried leaf basil
2 cups water
1/2 teaspoon salt
4 oz. fresh or frozen small shrimp,
    peeled, deveined

1/4 cup chili sauce
1/4 cup ketchup
1/2 tablespoon vinegar
2 drops Tabasco sauce
2 tablespoons minced celery
2 tablespoons minced onion
1 medium avocado

Prepare beans. In a medium bowl, combine beans, oil and basil. Stir to coat beans with oil. Bring water and salt to a boil in a small saucepan. Add shrimp. Bring water to a boil again and continue boiling 3 minutes; if using frozen precooked shrimp, let boil only 1 minute. Drain shrimp and rinse with cold water. Reserve 4 shrimp; stir remaining shrimp into bean mixture. In a small bowl, stir chili sauce, ketchup, vinegar, Tabasco sauce, celery and onion. Pour sauce over beans; stir to coat beans and shrimp. Peel avocado and cut into quarters. Place an avocado quarter on each of 4 salad plates. Fill avocado quarter with shrimp and bean mixture. Garnish with reserved shrimp. Serve immediately. Makes 4 servings.

Picnic Salad

Keep this salad—or any salad with mayonnaise—cold while transporting it to your picnic.

2 cups drained cooked Great Northern beans,
    page 15, or 1 (15-oz.) can cannellini
    beans, drained
1 qt. water
1 teaspoon salt
3/4 cup elbow macaroni
1/2 cup water
1/2 teaspoon salt
1 (10-oz.) pkg. frozen Italian green beans
1/2 cup sliced ripe olives

1/4 cup chopped pimiento
1 (6-oz.) jar marinated artichoke hearts
1/2 tablespoon lemon juice
1/8 teaspoon dried leaf oregano
1/8 teaspoon dried leaf basil
Pinch of dried dill weed
1/8 teaspoon salt
Pepper to taste
1 drop Tabasco
1/3 cup mayonnaise

Prepare beans. In a large saucepan, bring 1 quart water and 1 teaspoon salt to a boil. Add macaroni; reduce heat. Simmer uncovered until macaroni is tender, about 8 minutes. Drain macaroni and place in a medium bowl. Bring 1/2 cup water and 1/2 teaspoon salt to a boil in a medium saucepan. Add Italian green beans; reduce heat. Cover and simmer 5 minutes. Drain Italian green beans and add to macaroni. Stir in Great Northern beans or cannellini beans, olives and pimiento. Drain artichoke hearts, reserving marinade in a small bowl. Cut artichoke hearts in quarters and add to macaroni and bean mixture. Combine reserved artichoke marinade, lemon juice, oregano, basil, dill, salt, pepper and Tabasco. Beat with a whisk. Add mayonnaise. Beat until smooth. Pour over salad; toss. Refrigerate at least 2 hours before serving. Makes 6 servings.

Spring Garden Bowl

Fresh vegetables make this salad a spring delight, but you can use canned or frozen.

1/4 to 1/3 cup Creamy Herb Dressing,
   page 70
1 lb. fresh green beans
Water
1 cup shelled fresh green peas

1 cup fresh asparagus tips
1 cucumber, peeled, sliced
6 radishes, sliced
2 tablespoons chopped chives or green onions

Prepare Creamy Herb Dressing. Break fresh beans into 1-inch pieces. Steam over boiling water or boil in 1/2-cup water 10 minutes. Add fresh peas and fresh asparagus to green beans; steam or boil 10 minutes longer. Immediately plunge vegetables into a large bowl of cold water. When vegetables are cool, remove from water and dry on paper towels. In a salad bowl, combine cooked vegetables, cucumber, radishes and chives or green onions. Pour dressing over salad; toss lightly. Serve immediately or refrigerate until ready to serve. Makes 4 to 6 servings.

Variations

To make the salad with canned vegetables, do not cook the vegetables before tossing with the dressing. To use frozen vegetables, cook them according to the package directions before tossing with the dressing.

Turkey Toss

You can use chicken instead of turkey. Either way, this salad is better the second day.

1 cup water
1 chicken bouillon cube
Dash of garlic salt
Dash of onion salt
1/2 cup uncooked rice
2 cups mung bean sprouts or lentil sprouts
1 cup diced cooked turkey
1/2 cup diced celery
1/2 medium green pepper, diced
3 green onions, chopped

1 (6-oz.) jar marinated artichoke hearts
1/2 tablespoon lemon juice
1/8 teaspoon dried leaf oregano
1/8 teaspoon dried leaf basil
Pinch of dried dill weed
1/8 teaspoon salt
Black pepper to taste
1 drop of Tabasco sauce
1/2 teaspoon curry
1/3 cup mayonnaise

Bring water to a boil in a small saucepan. Add bouillon cube, garlic salt and onion salt; stir to dissolve. Slowly stir in rice. Reduce heat to lowest setting. Cover and simmer 20 minutes. Wash and drain sprouts in a colander. In a medium bowl, combine sprouts, turkey and cooked rice. Mix in celery, green pepper and green onions. Drain artichoke hearts, reserving marinade. Cut artichokes in quarters; add to salad. In a small bowl, combine reserved artichoke marinade, lemon juice, oregano, basil, dill weed, salt, black pepper, Tabasco sauce and curry. Beat with a whisk. Add mayonnaise. Beat until smooth. Pour over salad; fold to mix. Refrigerate at least 2 hours. Makes 4 servings.

Superb Taco Salad

To keep this avocado pieces fresh-looking, dip them in diluted lime or lemon juice.

2 cups Chili Beans, page 19, or
   1 (15-oz.) can ranch-style beans
1-1/2 cups Green Chili Salsa, page 69
4 tablespoons vegetable oil
1 teaspoon ground cumin
6 cups shredded lettuce

2 fresh medium tomatoes, diced
1 avocado, peeled, diced
1/2 cup sliced ripe olives
1 cup shredded Longhorn cheese
2 cups corn chips or tortilla chips

Prepare beans and Green Chili Salsa. In a small bowl, combine salsa, oil and cumin. Beat vigorously with a whisk. Arrange lettuce, beans, tomatoes, avocado and olives in a large salad bowl. Refrigerate until ready to serve. Add cheese and chips to salad before serving. Pour salsa over salad. Toss lightly. Makes 6 to 8 servings.

Curried Succotash

Try this delicious marinated salad with hamburgers, roasts or fried chicken.

1 cup water
1 teaspoon salt
1 (10-oz.) pkg. frozen corn
1 (10-oz.) pkg. frozen baby lima beans
1/2 cup chopped onion
1/3 cup chopped celery
1/3 cup chopped green pepper
1 tablespoon butter or margarine

1/3 cup diced pimiento
3 tablespoons honey
3/4 cup vinegar
1/3 cup water
2 teaspoons curry powder
4 whole cloves
1 (3-inch) cinnamon stick

Using 2 medium saucepans, bring 1/2 cup water and 1/2 teaspoon salt to a boil in each. Cook corn in one saucepan 5 minutes until thawed. Cook lima beans in second saucepan 10 minutes. Drain both vegetables and combine in a large bowl. In a small skillet, sauté onion, celery and green pepper in butter or margarine until onion is tender but not browned. Add sautéed vegetables and pimiento to beans and corn; mix well. In a small saucepan, combine honey, vinegar, water, curry, cloves and cinnamon stick. Bring to a boil; reduce heat. Cover and simmer 10 minutes. Strain marinade over salad; stir. Refrigerate 6 hours or overnight. Makes 8 to 10 servings.

Good Luck Platter

In the food lore of the South, eating black-eyed peas on New Year's Day brings good luck.

4 cups drained cooked black-eyed peas,
    page 15, or 2 (15-oz.) cans black-eyed
    peas, drained
1/4 cup chopped chives or green onions
1/4 cup vegetable oil

3 tablespoons lemon juice
1 teaspoon salt
Fresh spinach leaves, washed, stemmed
2 radishes, sliced

Prepare black-eyed peas. In a medium bowl, mix peas and chives, In a small jar or container with a tight-fitting lid, combine oil, lemon juice and salt. Shake vigorously about 1 minute. Pour dressing over peas. Stir gently to coat peas. Refrigerate 2 hours before serving. Arrange spinach leaves on a platter and spoon salad onto spinach leaves. Garnish with radish slices. Makes 4 to 6 servings. servings.

Pepperoni & Lentils

This spicy salad looks impressive and appetizing in a glass bowl.

1 cup dried lentils
1 sliver of lemon peel
1 small bay leaf
3 cups water
1 teaspoon salt
2 to 4 tablespoons Mustard French Dressing,
    page 69
3 oz. pepperoni, sliced

1/2 cup diced peeled cucumber
1 small tomato, diced
1/4 cup sliced ripe olives
2 tablespoons chopped fresh parsley
2 green onions, sliced
1/2 lemon, cut in wedges
1 medium tomato, cut in wedges
3 to 4 sprigs fresh parsley

Sort and rinse lentils. In a medium saucepan, combine lentils, lemon peel, bay leaf, water and salt. Bring to a boil; reduce heat. Cover and simmer until lentils are tender, about 30 minutes. Prepare Mustard French Dressing. Drain lentils; discard water and seasonings. In a salad bowl, combine cooked lentils, pepperoni, cucumber, diced tomato, olives, parsley and green onions. Pour dressing over salad. Toss lightly to coat all ingredients. Refrigerate at least 2 hours. Garnish with tomato and lemon wedges and sprigs of fresh parsley. Makes 4 to 6 servings.

Beans In Aspic

This tangy molded salad is especially pretty for a buffet.

1 (12-oz.) can V-8 juice
1 (3-oz.) pkg. lemon gelatin
1/2 teaspoon Tabasco sauce
1 tablespoon vinegar
1/3 cup water
1/3 cup slivered almonds

1/3 cup chopped celery
1 cup drained canned French-style
  green beans
2 tablespoons Green Mayonnaise, page 72
Lettuce leaves

Bring V-8 juice to a boil in a medium saucepan; remove from heat. Stir in gelatin until dissolved. Stir in Tabasco sauce, vinegar and water. Refrigerate until thickened to the consistency of unbeaten egg whites. Toast almonds in a heavy skillet over medium heat, stirring constantly. Remove partially thickened gelatin from refrigerator. Stir in celery, green beans and toasted almonds. Pour into a 4-cup mold. Refrigerate until firm. Prepare Green Mayonnaise. To unmold, run a knife around the edge of gelatin and place bottom of mold in 1 inch of warm water 5 seconds. Place a platter upside-down over mold. Invert both platter and mold; remove mold. Arrange lettuce leaves around salad. Top with a dollop of Green Mayonnaise. Makes 4 servings.

How To Make Beans In Aspic

1/Thickened gelatin dropped from a spoon should have the consistency of unbeaten egg whites. Stir celery, green beans and toasted almonds into thickened gelatin. Return to refrigerator until firm.

2/Run a knife around edge of mold. Place mold in 1 inch of warm water 5 seconds. Place the platter on top of mold and invert. Remove mold. Arrange lettuce leaves around and under aspic edges. Garnish with Green Mayonnaise.

Eggplant Salad

Try this salad and crisp bread sticks with your next Italian dinner.

1 cup drained cooked red kidney beans,
    page 15, or 1 (8-oz.) can red kidney
    beans, drained
1 cup drained cooked Great Northern beans,
    page 15, or 1/2 (15-oz.) can cannellini
    beans, drained
2 to 4 tablespoons Italian Dressing, see below
1 green onion, chopped

1 garlic clove, minced
1/3 cup chopped green pepper
2 tablespoons vegetable oil
1 cup cubed, peeled eggplant
    (about 1-inch cubes)
1 medium tomato, peeled, diced
1 tablespoon chopped fresh parsley

Italian Salad Dressing:
1/3 cup vegetable oil
2-1/2 tablespoons wine vinegar
1/4 teaspoon dried leaf oregano
1/4 teaspoon dried leaf basil

1/8 teaspoon dried dill weed
1/4 teaspoon salt
Pepper to taste
2 drops Tabasco sauce

Prepare red kidney beans, Great Northern beans and Italian Salad Dressing. In a medium bowl, combine beans and onion. Mix well. In a medium skillet, sauté garlic and green pepper in oil 1 minute. Add eggplant. Stir constantly over medium heat until eggplant browns slightly. Stir in tomato and parsley. Reduce heat. Cover and simmer 5 minutes. Stir eggplant and tomato mixture into beans. Pour dressing over and stir gently. Refrigerate 6 to 8 hours before serving. Makes 4 to 6 servings.

Italian Salad Dressing:
Combine all ingredients in a container with a tight-fitting lid. Shake vigorously about 1 minute. Can be stored in refrigerator 3 to 4 weeks. Makes about 1/2 cup of salad dressing.

Wilted Green Salad

Hot dressing adds flavor and slightly wilts the spinach.

4 cups fresh spinach leaves
1 (16-oz.) can French-style green beans
3 slices bacon
1/2 teaspoon sugar

1/4 cup cider vinegar
1/2 teaspoon salt
1/8 teaspoon pepper

Wash and stem spinach. Tear into bite-size pieces. Put spinach in a salad bowl. Drain beans and toss with spinach. In a medium skillet, fry bacon until crisp. Drain on paper towels. Crumble bacon over beans. Drain all but 2 tablespoons bacon drippings from skillet. Stir in sugar, vinegar, salt and pepper. Bring to a boil, stirring constantly. Pour hot dressing over salad. Toss lightly. Serve immediately. Makes 4 to 6 servings.

Salad Dressings & Sauces

Salad dressing makes the difference between a salad no one remembers and one that becomes famous. The salad dressings in this section make truly delicious salads. Try them as suggested in Salads, pages 52 to 66, and on some of your other favorite salads.

The sauces in this section are designed to bring out the flavor of cooked beans in various bean dishes. However, they are versatile basic sauces. Green Chili Salsa and Spicy Tomato Sauce are Mexican-type sauces to use on tacos and enchiladas as well as over meat loaves or vegetables. Marinara Sauce is an all-purpose Italian sauce that is especially good with pasta dishes and vegetables.

All the recipes in this section can be doubled and refrigerated or frozen with the exception of Green Chili Salsa. This Mexican sauce contains large pieces of tomato which do not freeze well.

FREEZING TIPS FOR SAUCES

• Cool the sauce before freezing it. Hot sauce will warm the air in the freezer and endanger the quality of the other frozen foods.

• When you pour a sauce into the freezer container, leave 1 to 2 inches at the top for expansion during freezing.

• To avoid spilling in the freezer, pour the cooled sauce into freezer bags that can be locked closed. Place the bags flat on a baking sheet until the sauce is frozen. The bags can then be stacked easily in your freezer. If you don't have this type of freezer bag, line a freezer container with a regular freezer bag. Pour in the cooled sauce and twist the bag closed. When the sauce is frozen, remove the bag from the container. The bag goes in the freezer and the container is free for another use. Sauces can also be frozen in plastic freezer containers.

• Label each container with the date and use the sauce within 3 to 4 months.

• To thaw and reheat the sauce, place the freezer bag or container in a pan of warm water for 5 to 10 minutes. When the sauce is partially thawed, empty it into a saucepan and heat it over low heat, stirring frequently.

• Taste the sauce after reheating it. You may need to adjust the seasoning. Salt, chili powder and onion often decrease in flavor when frozen.

Something To Celebrate

Chicken Tetrazzini
Lemon-Buttered Broccoli Spears
Orange-Bean Salad, page 53
With
Sweet & Sour Honey Dressing,
page 71
Apple Surprise Cake, page 154

Pizza Party

Antipasto Mold, page 139
Savory Bean Pizza, page 111
With
Pizza Marinara Sauce, page 72
Orange-Pineapple Sherbet
Sugar Wafers

Green Chili Salsa

A mild chili sauce for dipping tortilla chips or topping beans.

1 (16-oz.) can tomatoes, drained, or	2 teaspoons chili powder
4 medium fresh tomatoes	1/4 teaspoon ground cumin
1 (4-oz.) can diced or chopped green chilies	1/4 teaspoon dried leaf oregano
2 green onions, chopped	1/2 teaspoon salt
1 garlic clove, minced	

Dice tomatoes; if using fresh tomatoes, peel before dicing. In a medium saucepan, combine diced tomatoes, with remaining ingredients. Cover and simmer 10 minutes. Serve warm or chilled. Makes about 2 cups of sauce.

Thousand Island Dressing

Salad olives are broken pimiento-stuffed olives.

1 cup mayonnaise	2 tablespoons chopped salad olives
1/2 teaspoon Tabasco sauce	1 green onion, chopped
1 tablespoon pickle relish	1/4 cup chili sauce

Combine all ingredients in a small bowl. Stir well. Can be stored in refrigerator 1 to 2 weeks. Makes about 1-1/4 cups of salad dressing.

Mustard French Dressing

Try this with Pepperoni & Lentils, page 64.

3/4 cup vegetable oil	1/2 teaspoon salt
1/4 cup wine vinegar	1/4 teaspoon pepper
1 tablespoon Dijon-style mustard	

Combine all ingredients in a 1-pint container with a tight-fitting lid. Shake vigorously about 1 minute. Can be stored in refrigerator 3 to 4 weeks. Makes about 1 cup of salad dressing.

Green Bean Chow Chow, page 27, is top center. Arranged clockwise are Green Chili Salsa, Thousand Island Dressing and Mustard French Dressing.

Yogurt Mayonnaise

Spoon this refreshingly light and creamy dressing over fresh fruits and vegetables.

3/4 cup mayonnaise
2 tablespoons plain yogurt
1/2 teaspoon sugar

1/4 teaspoon salt
1 green onion, chopped

Combine all ingredients in a small bowl. Mix well with a whisk or fork. Can be stored in refrigerator 1 to 2 weeks. Makes about 3/4 cup of salad dressing.

Vinaigrette Dressing

This classic French dressing is easy to make and so versatile!

1/4 cup red wine vinegar
1/2 cup vegetable oil
2 tablespoons olive oil
1 garlic clove, minced

1/2 teaspoon salt
1/4 teaspoon pepper
1 green onion, chopped
3 tablespoons chopped fresh parsley

Combine all ingredients in a 1-pint jar with a tight-fitting screw top. Shake vigorously about 1 minute. Can be stored in refrigerator 1 to 2 weeks. Makes about 3/4 cup of salad dressing.

Creamy Green Dressing

A flavorful and creamy dressing to pour over Spring Garden Bowl, page 61.

2 tablespoons chopped fresh parsley
1/4 cup finely chopped spinach leaves
2 green onions, cut in 1-inch pieces
1 teaspoon prepared mustard

1 egg yolk
3 tablespoons vinegar
1/2 cup vegetable oil

Combine all ingredients in blender container. Whip until smooth and creamy, 2 to 3 minutes. Can be stored in refrigerator 1 to 2 weeks. Makes about 3/4 cup of salad dressing.

Sweet & Sour Honey Dressing

Especially good on Orange-Bean Salad, page 53.

1/4 cup honey
1 cup vinegar
1 teaspoon salt

1/4 teaspoon pepper
2 tablespoons chopped green onion with
    green top

Combine all ingredients in a 1-pint container with a tight-fitting lid. Shake vigorously about 3 minutes. Can be stored in refrigerator 1 to 2 weeks. Makes about 1-1/4 cups of salad dressing.

Tangy Lemon Dressing

A tasty marinade for fresh vegetables.

2 tablespoons grated lemon peel
1/4 cup lemon juice
1/2 cup vegetable oil
1 garlic clove, minced
1/4 teaspoon ground cumin

1/4 teaspoon dry mustard
1/4 teaspoon paprika
1/2 teaspoon salt
1/2 teaspoon sugar
1/8 teaspoon cayenne pepper

Combine all ingredients in a small container with a tight-fitting lid. Shake vigorously about 1 minute. Can be stored in refrigerator 3 to 4 weeks. Makes 3/4 cup of salad dressing.

Creole Dipping Sauce

Excellent for vegetable dippers, chips or Black-Eyed Fritters, page 21.

1 tablespoon finely chopped onion
1 garlic clove, minced
2 tablespoons finely chopped green pepper
1 tablespoon vegetable oil

1 (8-oz.) can tomato sauce
1/2 teaspoon salt
1/2 teaspoon sugar
1/4 teaspoon dried leaf thyme

In a small saucepan, sauté onion, garlic and green pepper in oil until onion is tender but not browned. Stir in remaining ingredients. Cover and simmer 10 minutes. Serve warm. Makes 1 cup of sauce.

Spicy Tomato Sauce

A peppy sauce to top meat loaf or toss with vegetables.

1 (15-oz.) can tomato sauce
1 garlic clove, minced
1/4 teaspoon dried leaf basil

1/2 teaspoon dried leaf oregano
1/4 teaspoon salt
1 teaspoon chili powder

Combine all ingredients in a medium saucepan. Bring to a boil; reduce heat. Cover and simmer 10 minutes. Serve hot. Makes about 2 cups of sauce.

Marinara Sauce

A quick, all-purpose Italian sauce.

1 tablespoon olive oil or other vegetable oil
1 garlic clove, minced
1 cup canned tomatoes and juice
1/4 teaspoon salt
Pepper to taste

1/4 teaspoon dried leaf oregano
Pinch of dried leaf basil
Pinch of sugar
1 tablespoon chopped fresh parsley

Heat oil in a medium saucepan. Sauté garlic in oil about 1 minute. Add remaining ingredients, breaking up tomatoes with a fork. Cover and simmer 10 minutes. Makes about 1 cup of sauce.

Variation

Pizza Marinara Sauce: To make a thicker sauce for pasta or pizza, stir 1 tablespoon tomato paste into tomato mixture before simmering 10 minutes.

Green Mayonnaise

Mayonnaise never tasted so good! Use it to dress-up Beans In Aspic, page 65.

1 cup mayonnaise
2 teaspoons lemon juice
2 tablespoons chopped parsley

2 tablespoons chopped green onion
1/4 cup chopped fresh spinach
1/4 teaspoon dried leaf tarragon

Combine all ingredients in a small bowl. Stir well. Refrigerate at least 6 hours before using. Can be stored in refrigerator 1 to 2 weeks. Makes about 1-1/4 cups of salad dressing.

Sesame Seed Dressing

Use this dressing the day you make it. It's delightful with Capistrano Sandwiches, page 31.

1 tablespoon sesame seeds	1 teaspoon prepared mustard
1/4 cup vinegar	1/2 teaspoon salt
1 tablespoon soy sauce	1 tablespoon chopped onion
1 tablespoon sugar	1/2 cup vegetable oil
1/8 teaspoon paprika	

In a small heavy skillet, stir sesame seeds over medium-high heat until golden, 3 to 5 minutes. Watch seeds carefully to prevent burning. Set seeds aside. In a small bowl, combine vinegar, soy sauce, sugar, paprika, mustard, salt and onion. Stir to dissolve sugar. Slowly add the oil while beating with a whisk or electric mixer. When all oil has been added, stir in toasted sesame seeds. Makes about 3/4 cup of salad dressing.

How To Make Sesame Seed Dressing

1/Toast sesame seeds in a heavy skillet over medium-high heat. Stir constantly because the seeds burn quickly. In 3 to 5 minutes the seeds will become golden brown.

2/Slowly add vegetable oil to the vinegar mixture while beating with a whisk. Adding the oil slowly makes a thicker dressing. Stir in toasted sesame seeds.

Bean Pots

Bean pots are beans with a definite sweet flavor. The sweeteners may be molasses, sugar, honey or maple syrup.

If you cook beans without soaking them, they will taste as if they had simmered all day in the oven. To shorten the cooking time for a bean pot recipe, soak the beans before cooking; see Soaking, pages 5 and 6. Then reduce the cooking water by about half. Check the beans frequently to be sure they are covered by cooking liquid. Beans will be tender in about half the specified cooking time.

Cook beans for a bean pot until they are not quite tender. If the beans are completely cooked before baking, they will be overcooked and mushy after baking.

While beans are baking, they should be covered with liquid. The amount of liquid needed to cover the beans varies with the size and shape of the casserole or bean pot. A shallow 2-quart casserole requires less liquid than a tall 2-quart casserole or bean pot. The amounts of liquid given in these recipes may need to be adjusted to the size of the pot used for baking. If the beans are covered by cooking liquid, there is enough liquid in the pot.

Acid retards the cooking of beans and prevents them from softening. In any recipe that includes acidic ingredients, such as tomatoes, vinegar or ketchup, the beans must be cooked before these flavorings are added. After the beans are cooked, acidic ingredients can be added and the dish baked in the oven.

Let's Go On A Picnic
Juicy Grilled Hamburgers
Sesame Seed Rolls
Lettuce
Tomato Slices
Southern-Style Baked Beans,
page 83
Green Bean Chow Chow, page 27
Homemade Strawberry Ice Cream

New England Bean Supper
Honey-Glazed Ham
Boston Baked Beans, page 83
Boston Brown Bread
Green Tomato Relish
Dilly Beans, page 30
Tossed Vegetable Salad
Apple Pie

Jamaican Bean Pot

So beans won't dry out while cooking, check them often and add hot water as needed.

1 lb. dried black beans
10 cups water
1/2 cup chopped onion
1 garlic clove, minced
1/2 cup sliced celery
1/2 cup sliced carrot
2 tablespoons vegetable oil
1 bay leaf

1-1/2 teaspoons salt
1/4 cup molasses
1/4 cup packed brown sugar
1/4 cup dark Jamaican rum
1 teaspoon dry mustard
Pinch of dried leaf thyme
2 tablespoons butter or margarine

Sort and rinse beans; do not soak. In a 4-quart pot, combine rinsed beans and water. In a medium skillet, sauté onion, garlic, celery and carrot in oil until onion is tender but not browned. Add sautéed vegetables, bay leaf and salt to beans; stir. Bring to a boil; reduce heat. Cover and simmer until beans are almost tender, 1-1/2 to 2 hours, checking several times. Add hot water as needed to keep beans just covered while cooking. Drain beans, reserving cooking liquid. Remove and discard bay leaf. Preheat oven to 300°F (150°C). In a small bowl, combine molasses, brown sugar, 2 tablespoons rum, dry mustard and thyme; mix well. Put beans in a 2-1/2-quart bean pot or casserole with a cover. Pour molasses mixture over beans; stir. Add enough reserved cooking liquid to just cover beans, about 1-1/2 cups. Cover and bake 2 hours. Uncover, dot with butter or margarine and bake 30 minutes longer. Stir in remaining 2 tablespoons rum just before serving. Makes 6 to 8 servings.

Swedish Bean Bake

Spicy and slightly sweet, their aroma is delightful!

2 cups dried red or pink beans
8 cups water
1 tablespoon vegetable oil
1-1/2 teaspoons salt

1 cinnamon stick
6 tablespoons brown sugar
1/4 cup cider vinegar
1/3 cup dark corn syrup

Sort and rinse beans; do not soak. In a 4-quart pot, combine rinsed beans, water, vegetable oil, salt and cinnamon stick. Bring to a boil; reduce heat. Cover and simmer until beans are almost tender, 1-1/2 to 2 hours, checking several times. Add hot water as needed to keep beans just covered while cooking. Drain beans, reserving cooking liquid. Preheat oven to 300°F (150°C). Put beans in a 2-quart casserole with a cover. Stir in brown sugar, vinegar, corn syrup and enough reserved cooking liquid to just cover beans, about 3/4 cup. Cover and bake 2 hours. Uncover and bake 30 minutes longer. Remove cinnamon stick before serving. Makes 6 to 8 servings.

Bourbon Baked Beans

You'll notice the robust flavor, but you won't be able to identify the ingredients!

2 cups dried pea beans or small white beans
8 cups water
1 bay leaf
1-1/2 teaspoons salt
2 slices bacon

1/2 cup chopped onion
1 garlic clove, minced
1/4 cup strong coffee
1/3 cup molasses
1/4 cup bourbon

Sort and rinse beans; do not soak. In a 4-quart pot, combine rinsed beans, water, bay leaf and salt. In a small skillet, fry bacon until crisp. Drain on paper towels. Sauté onion and garlic in bacon drippings until onion is tender but not browned. Add onion mixture to beans. Bring to a boil; reduce heat. Cover and simmer until beans are almost tender, 1-1/2 to 2 hours, checking several times. Add hot water as needed to keep beans just covered while cooking. Drain beans, reserving cooking liquid. Preheat oven to 300°F (150°C). In a 2-quart casserole with a cover, combine beans, coffee, molasses and bourbon. Stir well. Add enough reserved cooking liquid to just cover beans, about 1/2 cup. Cover and bake 2 hours. Uncover and bake 30 minutes longer. Makes 6 to 8 servings.

Vermont Bean Pot

Slightly sweet yet spicy.

2 cups dried pea beans or small white beans
8 cups water
4 slices bacon, diced
1/2 cup chopped onion
1-1/2 teaspoons salt

1/8 teaspoon pepper
1 teaspoon ground ginger
1/2 teaspoon ground allspice
2 tablespoons cider vinegar
2/3 cup maple syrup

Sort and rinse beans; do not soak. In a 4-quart pot, combine rinsed beans and water. In a medium skillet, fry bacon until crisp. Drain on paper towels. Sauté onion in bacon drippings until tender but not browned. Add sautéed onion and salt to beans. Bring bean mixture to a boil; reduce heat. Cover and simmer until beans are almost tender, 1-1/2 to 2 hours, checking several times. Add hot water as needed to keep beans just covered while cooking. Drain, reserving cooking liquid. Preheat oven to 300°F (150°C). Measure reserved cooking liquid. Add water if necessary to make 1-1/4 cups. Combine reserved cooking liquid, pepper, ginger, allspice, vinegar and maple syrup in skillet. Bring to a boil. In a 2-quart casserole with a cover, combine beans and boiled syrup mixture. Crumble bacon over top. Cover and bake 2 hours. Uncover and bake 30 minutes longer. Makes 6 to 8 servings.

Butter-Baked Limas

You can use margarine, but the beans won't have the same richness and heavenly flavor.

2 cups dried large lima beans	1/2 cup honey
8 cups water	1/4 cup butter
1 tablespoon vegetable oil	1/2 cup water
2 teaspoons salt	1 cup frozen whole pearl onions

Sort and rinse beans; do not soak. In a 4-quart pot, combine rinsed beans, water, oil and salt. Bring to a boil; reduce heat. Cover and simmer until beans are almost tender, 1 to 1-1/2 hours, checking several times. Add hot water as needed to keep beans just covered while cooking. Drain, reserving 1 cup cooking liquid. Preheat oven to 300°F (150°C). Put beans in a 2-quart casserole with a cover. In a small bowl, combine reserved cooking liquid, honey and butter. Stir until butter melts. Pour mixture over beans; stir. Cover and bake 1 hour. In a small saucepan, bring 1/2 cup water to a boil. Add onions. Bring water to a boil again; reduce heat. Cover and simmer 5 minutes; drain. Fold cooked onions into beans. Cover and bake 1 hour longer. Makes 6 to 8 servings.

How To Cook Butter-Baked Limas

1/Beans not covered with liquid while cooking will be tough. If cooking liquid has been absorbed or has evaporated, add just enough hot water to cover.

2/Cover beans and continue simmering. The cooking liquid absorbed by the beans as they simmer will make the beans moist and tender.

Orange Baked Beans

For the best flavor, use fresh orange juice or juice made from frozen concentrate.

2 cups dried pea beans, small white beans or
   Great Northern beans
8 cups water
1 tablespoon vegetable oil
2 teaspoons salt

1 cup tomato sauce
2 tablespoons ketchup
1/2 cup orange juice
6 tablespoons brown sugar
1/2 teaspoon Worcestershire sauce

Sort and rinse beans; do not soak. In a 4-quart pot, combine rinsed beans, water, oil and salt. Bring to a boil; reduce heat. Cover and simmer until beans are almost tender, 1-1/2 to 2 hours, checking several times. Add hot water as needed to keep beans just covered while cooking. Drain beans, reserving 3/4 cup cooking liquid. Preheat oven to 300°F (150°C). Put beans in a 2-quart casserole with a cover. In a small bowl, combine reserved cooking liquid, tomato sauce, ketchup, orange juice, brown sugar and Worcestershire sauce. Stir well. Pour sauce over beans; stir. Cover and bake 1 hour. Makes 6 to 8 servings.

Country-Style Baked Limas

To substitute prepared mustard for dry mustard, use 3 times as much prepared mustard.

2 cups dried large lima beans
8 cups water
4 oz. salt pork, diced
1 medium onion, cut in quarters
2 teaspoons salt

1 teaspoon Worcestershire sauce
1 tablespoon vinegar
1/4 teaspoon dry mustard
1/3 cup molasses
1/3 cup chili sauce

Sort and rinse beans; do not soak. In a 4-quart pot, combine rinsed beans, water, salt pork, onion and salt. Bring to a boil; reduce heat. Cover and simmer until beans are almost tender, 1 to 1-1/2 hours, checking several times. Add hot water as needed to keep beans just covered while cooking. Drain, reserving 1-1/4 cups cooking liquid. Preheat oven to 300°F (150°C). In a 2-quart casserole with a cover, stir beans, reserved cooking liquid, Worcestershire sauce, vinegar, dry mustard, molasses and chili sauce. Cover and bake 2 hours. Uncover and bake 30 minutes longer. Makes 6 to 8 servings.

Check beans often as they begin to get tender so they don't overcook.

Peachy Ginger Beans

Because the bean pot is to be baked 1 hour, slightly undercook the Savory White Beans.

2 cups Savory White Beans made with
  pea beans or small white beans, page 18
1/2 cup tomato sauce
2 tablespoons brown sugar

1/2 teaspoon ground ginger
1 teaspoon prepared mustard
1 cup drained peach slices

Prepare Savory White Beans. Drain, reserving 1/2 cup cooking liquid. Preheat oven to 275°F (135°C). In a 1-quart casserole with a cover, combine beans, reserved liquid, tomato sauce, brown sugar, ginger and mustard. Stir well. Arrange peach slices on top. Cover and bake 1 hour. Makes 4 servings.

Baked Lentils

Try this dish once and you'll enjoy lentils more often!

1 cup dried lentils
2-1/2 cups water
2 teaspoons vegetable oil
1/2 cup chopped onion

1 teaspoon salt
1 cup drained canned tomatoes
1/3 cup chopped green pepper
2 green onions, chopped

Sort and rinse lentils; drain. In a medium saucepan, combine rinsed lentils, water, oil, onion and salt. Bring to a boil; reduce heat. Cover and simmer until lentils are almost tender, about 30 minutes. Preheat oven to 300°F (150°C). Dice tomatoes. Combine lentils, cooking liquid, tomatoes, green pepper and green onions in a 1-quart baking dish. Bake uncovered 1 hour. Makes 4 servings.

Western Range Beans

Take these rich-tasting beans to a cook-out or picnic.

3 slices bacon
1 medium onion, sliced
1 garlic clove, minced
1/4 cup molasses
2 tablespoons brown sugar

2 tablespoons cider vinegar
2 teaspoons prepared mustard
1 (15-oz.) can pinto beans, drained
1 (16-oz.) can baked beans
1 (15-oz.) can red kidney beans, drained

Preheat oven to 300°F (150°C). In a medium skillet, fry bacon until crisp. Drain on paper towels. Sauté onion and garlic in bacon drippings until onion is slightly softened, 1 minute. Add molasses, brown sugar, vinegar and mustard to onion mixture. Stir well. In a 2-quart casserole with a cover, combine pinto beans, baked beans, kidney beans and onion mixture. Crumble bacon over beans. Stir to combine ingredients. Cover and bake 1 hour. Makes 6 to 8 servings.

Sweet & Sour Baked Beans

Slightly undercook the Savory White Beans. They will continue to cook while baking in the sauce.

2 cups Savory White Beans using
   pea beans or small white beans, page 18
1 (8-oz.) can pineapple chunks packed in juice
1 teaspoon cornstarch
1 tablespoon soy sauce

2 tablespoons vinegar
1/4 cup sugar
2 drops Tabasco sauce
1/2 medium green pepper,
   cut in 1" x 1/4" strips

Prepare Savory White Beans. Drain, reserving cooking liquid. Preheat oven to 275°F (135°C). Drain pineapple, reserving juice. Add reserved cooking liquid to juice to make 3/4 cup. Stir cornstarch into juice mixture. In a small saucepan, combine juice mixture, soy sauce, vinegar, sugar and Tabasco sauce. Stir constantly over medium heat until sauce boils. Remove from heat. Combine beans and green pepper strips and drained pineapple in a 1-quart casserole with a cover. Pour sauce over. Stir gently. Cover and bake 1 hour. Makes 4 servings.

Spanish Bean Pot

Golden corn, bright red tomatoes and green chilies make this a colorful side dish.

1 cup dried garbanzo beans
Water for soaking
2-1/2 cups water
1 tablespoon vegetable oil
1 teaspoon salt
1/2 cup chopped onion
1 garlic clove, minced

1/4 cup chopped green pepper
2 tablespoons butter or margarine
1 (16-oz.) can tomatoes, undrained, diced
1 (16-oz.) can whole-kernel corn, drained
1 (4-oz.) can diced or chopped green chilies
1/4 teaspoon dried leaf oregano
1/8 teaspoon ground cumin

Sort and soak beans; see How To Prepare Dried Beans, pages 5 and 6. Drain beans; discard soak water. In a medium saucepan, combine soaked beans, 2-1/2 cups water, oil and salt. Bring to a boil; reduce heat. Cover and simmer until beans are tender, 1 to 1-1/2 hours. Drain beans in a colander. Return drained beans to saucepan. In a medium skillet, sauté onion, garlic and green pepper in butter or margarine until onion is tender but not browned. Add tomatoes, corn, green chilies, oregano and cumin. Stir well. Add sautéed onion mixture to beans; stir. Cover and simmer 20 minutes. Makes 4 servings.

Variation

Use 1 (15-ounce) can garbanzo beans in place of 1 cup dried garbanzo beans. Do not soak or cook canned beans. Drain beans. Combine with sautéed onion mixture and remaining ingredients. Cover and simmer 20 minutes.

Pear & Lima Bake

Large lima beans are softer than small limas or Great Northerns, so they will cook faster.

2 cups dried large or baby lima beans or
    Great Northern beans
8 cups water
1 tablespoon vegetable oil
1-1/2 teaspoons salt

1 (16-oz.) can pear halves, packed in juice,
    undrained
1/2 cup butter or margarine
1/2 cup honey

Sort and rinse beans; do not soak. In a 4-quart pot, combine rinsed beans, water, oil and salt. Bring to a boil; reduce heat. Cover and simmer until beans are almost tender, 1-1/2 to 2 hours, checking several times. Add hot water as needed to keep beans just covered while cooking. Drain beans. Preheat oven to 300°F (150°C). Drain and slice pears, reserving juice. In a small saucepan, heat 1/2 cup pear juice, butter or margarine and honey, stirring until butter or margarine melts. In a 2-quart casserole with a cover, layer half of the beans and cover with a third of the honey mixture. Then layer half of the pear slices and cover with another third of the honey mixture. Repeat with remaining beans and honey mixture. Top with remaining pears. Cover and bake 1 to 2 hours, depending on the type of bean. Uncover and bake 30 minutes longer. Makes 6 to 8 servings.

Quick & Easy Bean Pot

Make this tasty dish on a day you can't stay at home to watch a bean pot.

2 slices bacon
1/3 cup chopped onion
1 (16-oz.) can pork and beans in tomato sauce
2 tablespoons chili sauce

1 tablespoon brown sugar
1 teaspoon Worcestershire sauce
1/2 teaspoon prepared mustard

Preheat oven to 300°F (150°C). In a medium skillet, fry bacon until crisp. Drain on paper towels. Sauté onion in bacon drippings until tender but not browned. In a 1-quart casserole with a cover, combine sautéed onion and beans. Stir in chili sauce, brown sugar, Worcestershire sauce and mustard. Crumble bacon over beans. Cover and bake 45 minutes. Makes 4 servings.

Boston Baked Beans

Serve with thick buttered slices of warmed Boston brown bread.

1 lb. dried pea beans or small white beans
Water for soaking
6 cups water
1 medium onion, sliced
4 oz. salt pork, cut in 4 pieces

1/2 cup molasses
3 tablespoons sugar
1 teaspoon dry mustard
1-1/2 teaspoons salt
1/4 teaspoon pepper

Sort and soak beans; see How To Prepare Dried Beans, pages 5 and 6. Drain beans; discard soak water. Preheat oven to 300°F (150°C). In a 4-quart pot, combine soaked beans and 6 cups water. Bring to a boil; reduce heat. Cover and simmer 10 minutes. Drain beans in a colander over a large bowl, reserving cooking liquid. In a 2-1/2-quart bean pot or casserole with a cover, layer beans, onion and salt pork. In a small bowl, combine molasses, sugar, dry mustard, salt, pepper and 1 cup reserved cooking liquid. Pour over beans. Add enough more reserved cooking liquid to cover beans. Cover and bake 4 to 6 hours until beans are tender, checking beans several times. Stir in reserved cooking liquid as needed to keep beans just covered while cooking. Makes 6 to 8 servings.

How To Make Boston Baked Beans

1/Spread 1/3 of the beans in the bottom of a casserole or bean pot. Place 1/3 of the onion slices and 2 pieces of salt pork on top of beans. Repeat layers, then top with remaining beans.

2/Mix the molasses, sugar, seasonings and 1 cup of reserved cooking liquid in a bowl. Pour the molasses mixture over beans. Add reserved cooking liquid to cover beans. Cover and bake 4 to 6 hours.

Burgundy Baked Beans

Hearty Burgundy wine adds rich flavor and color.

2 cups dried red beans	2 teaspoons salt
8 cups water	3/4 cup Burgundy wine
1 tablespoon vegetable oil	3/4 cup packed brown sugar
1/2 cup chopped onion	1/4 cup dairy sour cream, if desired

Sort and rinse beans; do not soak. In a large saucepan, combine rinsed beans, water, oil, onion and salt. Bring to a boil; reduce heat. Cover and simmer until beans are almost tender, 1-1/2 to 2 hours, checking several times. Add hot water as needed to keep beans just covered while cooking. Drain beans, reserving cooking liquid. Preheat oven to 300°F (150°C). In a 2-quart casserole with a cover, combine beans, wine, brown sugar and enough reserved cooking liquid to just cover beans, about 3/4 cup. Stir well. Cover and bake 2 hours. Uncover and bake 30 minutes longer. If desired, serve with a dollop of sour cream or serve sour cream separately. Makes 6 to 8 servings.

Southern-Style Baked Beans

The South has its distinctive style of baking beans, too. This bean pot is pictured on the cover.

1 lb. dried pea beans or small white beans	1/4 cup molasses
10 cups water	1/3 cup ketchup
1 tablespoon vegetable oil	1 tablespoon prepared mustard
1 medium onion, sliced	1 teaspoon Worcestershire sauce
1-1/2 teaspoons salt	1/2 teaspoon ground ginger
1 bay leaf	4 oz. salt pork, thinly sliced
1 small red pepper, if desired	2 tablespoons brown sugar

Sort and rinse beans; do not soak. In a 4-quart pot, combine rinsed beans, water, oil, onion, salt, bay leaf and red pepper, if desired. Bring to a boil; reduce heat. Cover and simmer until beans are almost tender, 1-1/2 to 2 hours, checking beans several times. Add hot water as needed to keep beans just covered while cooking. Drain beans, reserving 1 cup cooking liquid. Remove and discard bay leaf and red pepper. Preheat oven to 300°F (150°C). In a small bowl, combine reserved cooking liquid, molasses, ketchup, mustard, Worcestershire sauce and ginger; mix well. Put beans in a 2-1/2-quart bean pot or casserole with a cover. Pour molasses mixture over beans; stir well. Arrange salt pork on top. Sprinkle top with brown sugar. Cover and bake 2 hours. Makes 6 to 8 servings.

Stews

Most of the bean stews in this book are complete meals. Serving them with crusty bread or a cool crisp salad adds a finishing touch.

Stews fit any occasion. If it's a family supper, ladle hearty portions of Appalachian Okra Stew into bowls directly from the stove. Spicy Beans & Ribs look especially appetizing in individual bean pot casseroles. Heavy mugs add a gourmet touch to Texas Chili With Beans, and gratin dishes make Louisiana Red Beans look elegant.

RICHLY FLAVORED BEANS

Cooking beans with smoked, cured meats, such as ham shanks, hocks or bacon, is an inexpensive way to add protein and rich flavor.

Shanks are the hind legs of swine. They are meaty and weigh 1 to 1-1/4 pounds. When fresh, they are called *pork shanks*; when cured, they are *ham shanks*. Smoked and cured, they are *smoked ham shanks* which are tastier than other shanks and add richer flavor to beans. However, shanks in any form add flavor. When using the less flavorful pork shanks, add 2 or 3 slices of bacon.

Look for shanks in meat markets and local grocery stores. You may have to order them. Have the butcher cut them into 3 or 4 pieces so more flavor will cook into the beans. If shanks are rare in your area, buy extra when you can and freeze them for future use.

For directions on removing meat from cooked shanks, see page 93.

Hocks are the front legs of swine. They weigh 3/4 to 1 pound. Fresh ham hocks are called *pork hocks*; when cured, they are *ham hocks*. If they are smoked after curing, they will be labelled *smoked ham hocks*. Hocks have a heavier layer of skin and fat than shanks and the meat is laced with gristle. There will be very little meat to cut from the bones and put back into the beans. To enhance their flavor, add 2 or 3 slices of bacon to the beans and hocks while they are cooking.

Hearty Supper
Massachusetts Settler's Succotash,
page 88
Bean Bonanza, page 57
Parsley-Buttered Toast Squares
Pumpkin Custard

Family Favorites
Old-Fashioned Beans & Ham,
page 93
Creamy Vegetable Toss, page 56
Southern Cornbread
With
Whipped Honey Butter
Warm Cherry Cobbler

Brunswick Stew

Rabbit was used in the early versions of this Southern stew.

1 (3-lb.) frying chicken or rabbit, cut up	1/2 teaspoon dried leaf oregano
4 cups water	2 medium potatoes, peeled, diced
1 large onion, sliced	1 (10-oz.) pkg. frozen baby lima beans
2 chicken bouillon cubes	1 (16-oz.) can tomatoes, undrained, diced
1/8 teaspoon cayenne pepper	1 (10-oz.) pkg. frozen whole-kernel corn
2 teaspoons Worcestershire sauce	1 teaspoon salt
1/4 teaspoon dried leaf thyme	2 slices white bread

In a 4-quart pot, combine chicken or rabbit pieces, water, onion, bouillon cubes, cayenne pepper, Worcestershire sauce, thyme and oregano. Bring to a boil; reduce heat. Cover and simmer until chicken or rabbit is tender, about 45 minutes. Remove chicken or rabbit pieces; set aside. Add potatoes and lima beans to boiling broth in pot. Cover and simmer until potatoes are tender, about 20 minutes. Add tomatoes, corn and salt. Add chicken or rabbit pieces to pot. Cover and simmer 10 minutes longer. Break bread into bite-size pieces. Add to stew; stir constantly until stew has thickened. For each serving, put a piece of chicken or rabbit in a large soup bowl. Surround with stew. Makes 6 servings.

Texas Chili With Beans

Chili powder—not tomatoes—gives this stew its red color.

2 cups cooked Western Beans, page 17	3 tablespoons all-purpose flour
1 (3-lb.) chuck roast	2 (10-1/2-oz.) cans beef broth
2 tablespoons vegetable oil	1/2 teaspoon dried leaf oregano
4 to 6 tablespoons chili powder	2 garlic cloves, minced
2 teaspoons ground cumin	1 teaspoon salt

Prepare Western Beans. While beans are cooking, bone chuck roast, remove fat and cut meat into 1/2-inch cubes. In a large skillet, heat 1 tablespoon oil. Add about 1/3 of the meat and brown well. Remove meat from skillet and set aside. Drain or spoon any excess juices from skillet. Continue browning 1/3 of the meat at a time, adding remaining oil as needed. Return all meat to skillet. In a small bowl, stir chili powder, cumin and flour. Sprinkle over meat; toss to coat. Stir in beef broth. Add oregano, garlic and salt. Bring to a boil; reduce heat. Cover and simmer until meat is tender, about 1-1/2 hours. Add beans including liquid. Simmer 30 minutes. Serve piping hot in large mugs. Makes 4 to 6 servings.

Cuban Black Beans & Rice

Cubans like spicy hot foods, but you can season to your taste by adding less red pepper.

1 lb. dried black beans
Water for soaking
1 cup chopped onion
1 tablespoon butter or margarine
4 cups water
1 beef bouillon cube
1 (1-lb.) ham shank, cut in 3 or 4 pieces
2 bay leaves
1/2 teaspoon dried leaf thyme
1/2 teaspoon dried leaf oregano

1/2 teaspoon salt
1 dried whole red pepper or 1/8 teaspoon
   cayenne pepper, if desired
3 cups uncooked rice
Water
Salt
1 cup chopped green pepper
1/3 cup dark rum, if desired
1 cup dairy sour cream, if desired

Sort and soak beans; see How To Prepare Dried Beans, pages 5 and 6. Drain beans; discard soak water. In a 4-quart pot, sauté onion in butter or margarine until tender but not browned. Add soaked beans, 4 cups water, bouillon cube, ham shank pieces, bay leaves, thyme, oregano, salt and red pepper or cayenne pepper, if desired. Bring to a boil; reduce heat. Cover and simmer until beans are tender, 1 to 1-1/2 hours. Cook rice with water and salt according to package directions. Remove 1 cup beans from stew. Mash in a small bowl with a potato masher or fork. Add mashed beans to stew; stir to thicken. Remove ham shank pieces and red pepper, if used. Discard red pepper. Cut meat from bones and discard bones. Dice meat. Add diced meat, green pepper and rum, if desired, to beans. Cover and simmer 15 minutes. Serve beans over rice. Top each serving with a dollop of sour cream, if desired. Makes 4 to 6 servings.

Massachusetts Settler's Succotash

The original version was made with dried corn, or hominy, and beans.

2 cups dried pea beans or small white beans
Water for soaking
5 cups water
1 chicken leg including thigh
1 chicken bouillon cube
1 teaspoon salt
8 oz. corned beef, cut in strips

1 cup sliced carrots
1 medium onion, sliced
1/4 teaspoon dried leaf thyme
1/4 teaspoon dried leaf oregano
1 medium potato, peeled, diced
1 (15-oz.) can golden hominy, drained

Sort and soak beans; see How To Prepare Dried Beans, pages 5 and 6. Drain beans; discard soak water. In a 4-quart pot, combine 5 cups water, soaked beans, chicken, bouillon cube, salt, corned beef, carrot, onion, thyme and oregano. Bring to a boil; reduce heat. Cover and simmer 30 minutes. Remove chicken. Cut meat from bones and discard bones. Dice meat; set aside. Add potato to bean mixture. Simmer 1 hour longer. Add hominy and diced chicken. Simmer 15 minutes. Serve steaming hot in large soup bowls. Makes 4 to 6 servings.

Louisiana Red Beans & Rice

In Louisiana tradition, Sunday dinner's ham bone provides the meat and flavor.

1 lb. dried red beans
Water for soaking
1 tablespoon vegetable oil
2 green onions, chopped
1/2 cup chopped onion
1/4 cup chopped celery leaves
2 garlic cloves, minced
5 cups water

1 teaspoon salt
1/4 teaspoon pepper
1/8 to 1/4 teaspoon Tabasco sauce
1 (1-lb.) ham shank, cut in 3 or 4 pieces
3 cups uncooked rice
Water
Salt
1/2 cup chopped green onions

Sort and soak beans; see How To Prepare Dried Beans, pages 5 and 6. Drain beans; discard soak water. In a 4-quart pot, heat oil over moderate heat. Add 2 chopped green onions, white or yellow onion, celery leaves and garlic. Sauté until onion is tender but not browned. Add beans, 5 cups water, 1 teaspoon salt, pepper and Tabasco sauce. Stir well. Bury ham shank pieces in beans. Bring beans to a boil; reduce heat. Cover and simmer until beans are tender, 1 to 1-1/2 hours. Cook rice with water and salt according to package directions. Remove about 1 cup of beans; mash with a potato masher. Return mashed beans to pot. Remove ham shank pieces. Cut meat from bones and discard bones. Dice meat. Add diced meat to beans. Serve beans over hot rice with a generous sprinkling of chopped green onions. Makes 4 to 6 servings.

Chili Gumbo

Gumbo filé is crushed dried wild sassafras. Look for it in your local gourmet shop.

3/4 cup dried black-eyed peas
1 tablespoon bacon drippings or lard
2 cups water
1/2 teaspoon salt
1/2 lb. ground beef
1 cup chopped onion
2 garlic cloves, minced
1 (16-oz.) can tomatoes, undrained, chopped

1 (4-oz.) can diced or chopped green chilies
1 bay leaf
1 teaspoon chili powder
3/4 teaspoon ground cumin
1/2 teaspoon salt
1 (10-1/2-oz.) can beef broth
1 (10-oz.) pkg. frozen cut okra
1/2 teaspoon gumbo filé

Sort and rinse black-eyed peas. In a medium saucepan, combine peas, bacon drippings or lard, water and 1/2 teaspoon salt. Bring to a boil; reduce heat. Cover and simmer until peas are tender, 1 to 1-1/2 hours. In a 4-quart heavy pot, brown beef until it is no longer pink. Spoon excess fat from pot. Add onion and garlic. Cook and stir 2 to 3 minutes. Stir in tomatoes, green chilies, bay leaf, chili powder, cumin and 1/2 teaspoon salt. Cover and simmer 15 minutes. Add black-eyed pea mixture and okra. Cover and simmer 15 minutes. Remove 1/2 cup liquid from stew. Stir gumbo filé into liquid. Add gumbo filé mixture to stew. Simmer 3 minutes, stirring constantly. Serve immediately; overcooked gumbo filé causes soup to become stringy. Makes 6 servings.

Appalachian Okra Stew

Okra's green pods contribute their own thickening agent to soups and sauces.

1/2 (3-lb.) frying chicken	1/2 cup chopped celery
1 (1-lb.) meaty ham shank, cut in 3 or 4 pieces	1 (10-oz.) pkg. frozen lima beans
4 cups water	2 teaspoons Worcestershire sauce
3/4 cup sliced carrots	1 teaspoon salt
1 cup chopped onion	4 drops Tabasco sauce
3/4 cup diced green pepper	1 (10-oz.) pkg. frozen sliced okra

In a heavy 4-quart pot, combine chicken, ham shank, water, carrots, onion, green pepper, celery, lima beans, Worcestershire sauce, salt and Tabasco sauce. Bring to a boil; reduce heat. Cover and simmer 1 hour. Remove chicken and ham shank. Cut meat from bones and discard bones. Dice meat. Add diced chicken and ham to stew. Add frozen okra, breaking apart with a fork as it thaws. Simmer 30 minutes longer. Serve in large soup bowls. Makes 4 to 6 servings.

Lamb Stew

Inexpensive lamb shanks give rich flavor to beans and vegetables.

1 cup dried garbanzo beans	2 (10-1/2-oz.) cans beef broth
Water for soaking	1/2 cup water
2 lbs. lamb shanks, cut in 2 or 3 pieces	1 bay leaf
1 tablespoon vegetable oil	1/2 teaspoon dried leaf thyme
1 medium onion, sliced	1 teaspoon salt
1 carrot, sliced	1/2 teaspoon pepper
2 garlic cloves, minced	2 medium zucchini, thinly sliced
1/2 cup sliced celery	12 cherry tomatoes, peeled, see opposite page

Sort and soak beans; see How To Prepare Dried Beans, pages 5 and 6. Drain beans; discard soak water. In a medium skillet, brown lamb shanks in oil. Remove browned shanks and set aside. Sauté onion, carrot, garlic and celery in drippings until onion is tender but not browned. In a 4-quart pot, combine soaked beans, browned lamb shanks, sautéed vegetables, broth, 1/2 cup water, bay leaf, thyme, salt and pepper. Bring to a boil; reduce heat. Cover and simmer until beans and lamb are tender, 1 to 1-1/2 hours. Add zucchini. Cover and cook 10 minutes. Stir in tomatoes. Simmer 5 minutes longer. Serve in soup bowls. Makes 4 servings.

Variation

Use 1 (15-ounce) can garbanzo beans in place of 1 cup dried garbanzo beans. Do not soak or cook canned beans. Drain beans. Cook lamb with vegetables until tender, then add beans. Cover and cook 10 minutes before adding tomatoes.

Cholent

A traditional slow-cooked Jewish stew.

2 cups dried pinto beans
Water for soaking
1 to 2 tablespoons vegetable oil
2 garlic cloves, minced
1-1/2 lbs. beef short ribs, cut in 2-inch pieces
1 cup chopped onion
5 cups water

2 beef bouillon cubes
1/2 cup barley
1 large potato, peeled, diced
2 teaspoons salt
1/4 teaspoon pepper
2 teaspoons paprika

Sort and soak beans; see How To Prepare Dried Beans; pages 5 and 6. Drain beans; discard soak water. In a large skillet, heat 1 tablespoon oil and garlic. Brown short ribs in oil on all sides. Remove ribs; set aside. Add remaining 1 tablespoon oil if needed. Sauté onion until softened. In a heavy 4-quart pot, bring 5 cups water and bouillon cubes to a boil, stirring to dissolve bouillon. Add soaked beans, sautéed onion, barley, potato, salt, pepper and paprika to bouillon. Stir well. Sink ribs into beans. Bring to a boil; reduce heat. Cover and simmer 2 hours. Put 1 or 2 pieces of ribs in individual gratin dishes or bowls. Ladle bean mixture over ribs. Makes 6 to 8 servings.

How To Peel Cherry Tomatoes
For Lamb Stew

1/Because cherry tomato skins are tough, it's best to peel them. Put cherry tomatoes in a colander. Place in a large bowl. Pour boiling water over tomatoes to cover. Let stand 30 seconds in hot water.

2/Lift the colander from the bowl. Discard water. Cover tomatoes with cold water. Pierce the skin of each tomato with the point of a knife, then peel. Remove the blossom end before adding tomatoes to the stew.

Spicy Beans & Ribs

Start with 1 tablespoon of chili powder; add more to taste. Cayenne pepper makes it hotter still.

2 cups dried kidney beans
Water for soaking
2 lbs. beef short ribs, cut in 2-inch pieces
1 (10-3/4-oz.) can beef broth
4 cups water
2 slices bacon, diced
3/4 cup chopped onion

2 garlic cloves, minced
1 to 2 tablespoons chili powder
2 tablespoons cider vinegar
1 tablespoon brown sugar
2 cups tomato juice
1/8 teaspoon cayenne pepper, if desired
1 teaspoon salt

Sort and soak beans; see How To Prepare Dried Beans, pages 5 and 6. Drain beans; discard soak water. In a 4-quart pot, combine soaked beans, ribs, broth and 4 cups water. Bring to a boil; reduce heat. Cover and simmer until beans are tender, 1 to 1-1/2 hours. In a medium skillet, fry bacon until crisp. Drain on paper towels. Sauté onion and garlic in bacon drippings until onion is tender but not browned. Stir in chili powder, vinegar, brown sugar, tomato juice and cayenne pepper, if desired. Stir and simmer 5 minutes. Add tomato juice mixture to beans. Stir in salt. Cover and simmer 15 minutes. Put 2 or 3 pieces of ribs in individual bean pots or soup bowls. Cover with beans and sauce. Makes 4 to 6 servings.

Beefy Burgundy Beans

Burgundy brings out the rich flavor and color of the beans.

4 cups cooked Western Beans, page 17
1 lb. lean ground beef
1/8 teaspoon pepper
1 teaspoon salt
1 cup chopped onion
1 garlic clove, minced
3 tablespoons all-purpose flour
1 (10-1/2-oz.) can beef broth

1-1/2 cups Burgundy wine
1 tablespoon tomato paste
1/2 teaspoon dried leaf thyme
1 bay leaf
1 (8-oz.) pkg. noodles, cooked
Water
Salt

Prepare Western Beans; drain. In a large skillet, brown beef until no longer pink. Spoon off all but about 1 tablespoon drippings. Season cooked beef with pepper and 1 teaspoon salt. Add onion and garlic. Stir and cook until onion is softened. Sprinkle flour over meat mixture; stir to mix. Stir in broth, wine and tomato paste. Add drained beans, thyme and bay leaf. Mix well. Cover and simmer 30 minutes. Cook noodles with water and salt according to package directions. Place cooked noodles in individual casseroles or shallow soup bowls. Ladle generous amounts of beans over noodles. Makes 6 to 8 servings.

Old-Fashioned Beans & Ham

Grandma's favorite stew used ham ends and bones. She served it with hot biscuits.

2 cups dried large lima beans	3 bay leaves
Water for soaking	1 (1-lb.) ham shank, cut in 3 or 4 pieces
4 slices bacon, diced	3-1/2 cups water
1 cup chopped onion	1 teaspoon salt

Sort and soak lima beans; see How To Prepare Dried Beans, pages 5 and 6. Drain lima beans; discard soak water. Put soaked lima beans in a 4-quart pot. In a medium skillet, fry bacon until almost crisp. Add onion and continue cooking until onion is tender but not browned. Add bacon-onion mixture to lima beans. Break bay leaves in half and add to beans. Add ham shank pieces, 3-1/2 cups water and salt. Bring to a boil; reduce heat. Cover and simmer until beans are tender, about 45 minutes. Remove from heat and cool at least 1 hour at room temperature or overnight in refrigerator. Remove pieces of ham. Cut meat from bones and discard bones. Dice meat. Add diced ham to beans. Remove and discard bay leaves. To serve, reheat stew uncovered over medium-low heat until heated through, 20 to 30 minutes, stirring frequently to prevent sticking. Serve in rimmed plates or shallow soup bowls. Makes 4 to 6 servings.

How To Remove Meat From A Ham Shank
For Old-Fashioned Beans & Ham

1/Remove pieces of ham shank from beans. Using a paring knife and a fork, cut meat away from bones. Discard bones.

2/Trim excess fat from meat, then dice the meat. Stir diced meat into beans.

Pioneer Stew

If dried garbanzo beans aren't available, use canned garbanzos and follow the variation below.

1 cup dried red kidney beans	1/2 cup chopped onion
1 cup dried garbanzo beans	3/4 teaspoon dried leaf oregano
Water for soaking	1/2 teaspoon dried leaf basil
1/2 (3-lb.) frying chicken	Pinch of dried leaf thyme
7 cups water	1 teaspoon salt
4 chicken bouillon cubes	1 tablespoon chopped fresh parsley
1 dried red pepper	2 tablespoons uncooked rice
1 bay leaf	

Sort and soak dried beans; see How To Prepare Dried Beans, pages 5 and 6. Drain beans; discard soak water. In a 4-quart pot, combine chicken, 7 cups water, bouillon, red pepper, bay leaf, soaked beans, onion, oregano, basil, thyme, salt and parsley. Cover and simmer until chicken is tender, about 30 minutes. Remove chicken. Cut meat from bones and discard bones. Dice meat. Continue simmering beans until almost tender, 15 minutes. Add rice. Simmer 20 minutes. Add diced chicken; simmer 10 minutes. Serve in large soup mugs or bowls. Makes 6 to 8 servings.

Variation

Use 1 (15-ounce) can dark red kidney beans in place of 1 cup dried kidney beans, and 1 (15-ounce) can garbanzo beans in place of 1 cup dried garbanzo beans. Drain canned beans. Do not soak or cook. Reduce water from 7 cups to 3 cups. Reduce bouillon cubes from 4 to 2. Cook chicken with flavorings as directed above. Add beans to cooking liquid with rice before simmering 20 minutes. Add chicken as directed.

Cowpuncher Stew

Imported from the Mediterranean area, pungent cumin is available ground or as seeds.

2 cups drained, cooked pinto beans, page 15, or 1 (15-oz.) can pinto beans, drained	1 (16-oz.) can tomatoes, undrained
	1 (4-oz.) can diced or chopped green chilies
2 tablespoons vegetable oil	5 cups water
1 lb. lean beef, cut in 1/2-inch cubes	3 beef bouillon cubes
1 lb. lean pork, cut in 1/2-inch cubes	1 teaspoon cumin seeds
1 cup chopped onion	2 medium potatoes, peeled, cubed
2 garlic cloves, minced	1 (16-oz.) can cut green beans
	Salt to taste

Prepare pinto beans. Heat oil in a large skillet. Add beef and pork cubes. Stir over medium heat until meat is browned. Stir in onion and garlic. Cook 2 minutes or until onion is softened. In a 4-quart pot, combine browned meat mixture, tomatoes, green chilies, water, bouillon cubes and cumin seeds. Break up tomatoes with a fork. Bring mixture to a boil; reduce heat. Cover and simmer until meat is tender, 1 to 1-1/2 hours. Add pinto beans, potatoes, green beans and salt to taste. Simmer 30 minutes longer. Makes 6 to 8 servings.

Casseroles

To make a casserole, combine a high protein food, such as meat, cheese or beans, with rice, pasta or potatoes and one or more vegetables. Toss it all with a sauce, then bake it, and you've got an easy, filling and tasty meal. A beverage and dessert are all you need to complete it. For a hot lunch or a light supper, consider serving a casserole. Ham Casserole Amandine and Curried Chicken & Noodles won't disappoint you.

A casserole can be prepared in advance and refrigerated. An hour before dinner you can pop it in the oven and spend that hour relaxing or creating a sensational salad or dessert.

Casseroles are economical—especially when you use beans. They are inexpensive and can be used as satisfying budget stretchers. It takes only a little meat to give beans their complete protein value; see Protein, pages 2 and 3. One half pound of ground beef or sausage serves 4 to 6 people when it's combined with beans. You'll see what we mean when you try Beef & Biscuit Casserole or Bean & Sausage Bake. Another way to stretch both protein and your budget is to combine beans with cheese, eliminating meat altogether! Tomato-Lima Bake and Beans & Cheese are delicious, meatless meals.

Easy Family Get-Together
Ham Casserole Amandine, page 99
Apple-Bean Slaw, page 53
Date-Bran Muffins
Chocolate Pudding
With
Minted Whipped Topping

Supper With A Festive Flair
Nachos, page 24
Fiesta Casserole, page 97
Lettuce & Sliced Tomato Salad
With
Guacamole
Caramel Flan

Fiesta Casserole

Layer beans and beef with a spicy tomato sauce, tortillas and cheese.

2 cups drained, cooked pinto beans,
    page 15, or 1 (15-oz.) can pinto beans
    drained
1/2 lb. ground beef
1/2 cup chopped onion
1 teaspoon salt
1/4 teaspoon pepper
1 (28-oz.) can tomatoes, undrained, diced
1 (4-oz.) can diced or chopped green chilies

1 garlic clove, minced
1/2 teaspoon ground cumin
2 teaspoons chili powder
1/2 teaspoon dried leaf oregano
1 (8-oz.) can tomato sauce
6 corn tortillas
Oil for frying
2 cups shredded Longhorn Cheddar cheese

Prepare pinto beans. In a large skillet, brown ground beef until no longer pink. Drain all but about 1 tablespoon drippings. Push beef to one side. Sauté onion in remaining drippings until tender but not browned. Stir onion, salt and pepper into beef. Add beans; stir. In a medium saucepan, combine tomatoes, green chilies, garlic, cumin, chili powder, oregano and tomato sauce. Bring to a boil; reduce heat. Cover and simmer 10 minutes. Preheat oven to 350°F (175°C). Fry tortillas in 1/2-inch of oil in a medium skillet only until softened. Drain on paper towels. Spread a thin layer of sauce on the bottom of a 2-quart rectangular baking pan. Top with 3 tortillas, overlapping as necessary. Spread half the bean-beef mixture over tortillas. Pour sauce over to cover. Sprinkle with half the cheese. Repeat layers with remaining ingredients, ending with a layer of cheese. Bake 30 minutes. Cut into 4 or 6 rectangles. Serve with a spatula. Makes 4 to 6 servings.

Potato Scallop

Inexpensive beans and potatoes stretch half a pound of ground beef to serve four.

2 cups drained, cooked red kidney beans,
    page 15, or 1 (15-oz.) can red kidney beans,
    drained
1/2 lb. lean ground beef
1 medium onion, sliced
1/2 teaspoon salt

Pepper to taste
2 tablespoons butter or margarine
2 tablespoons all-purpose flour
1/2 teaspoon salt
2-1/2 cups milk, warmed
3 medium potatoes, sliced

Prepare beans; drain. Preheat oven to 350°F (175°C). In a medium skillet, brown beef until no longer pink. Add onion. Cook and stir until onion is tender but not browned. Spoon off any excess drippings. Sprinkle meat mixture with 1/2 teaspoon salt and pepper; set aside. In a medium saucepan, melt butter or margarine. Stir in flour and 1/2 teaspoon salt until smooth. Gradually add warm milk, stirring until smooth. Stir constantly over medium heat until mixture thickens and comes to a boil; set aside. In a 3-quart casserole, layer one-third of the potato slices, half of the beef and onion mixture and half of the beans. Pour about a third of the thickened sauce over layers. Repeat layers ending with potato slices. Top with remaining sauce. Bake uncovered until potato slices are tender and crusty brown on top, about 1 hour. Serve bubbling hot. Makes 4 servings.

Tomato-Lima Bake

Use the remaining canned tomatoes in Soybean Puree With Vegetables, page 42.

4 cups Savory White Beans made with
  large lima beans, page 18
1 cup canned tomatoes, undrained, diced
1 (8-oz.) can tomato sauce (1 cup)
1/2 teaspoon dried leaf basil

1/2 teaspoon salt
1/8 teaspoon black pepper
1 cup diced green pepper
1 cup diced Swiss cheese

Prepare Savory White Beans. Drain beans. Preheat oven to 350°F (175°C). In a 2-quart casserole, combine drained beans, tomatoes, tomato sauce, basil, salt and black pepper. Stir well. Stir in green pepper and cheese. Bake uncovered 45 minutes. Makes 4 to 6 servings.

Grandma's Sausage & Sauerkraut

Black rye bread and a fresh spinach salad complete this savory supper.

2 cups dried pinto beans
Water for soaking
2 tablespoons lard or bacon drippings
1 garlic clove, minced
5 cups water
1-1/2 teaspoons salt

1/2 lb. bulk pork sausage
1 cup chopped onion
1 (16-oz.) can sauerkraut, drained
1/4 teaspoon pepper
4 oz. smoky sausage links, cut in 1-inch pieces
1 (10-1/2-oz.) can beef broth

Sort and soak beans; see How To Prepare Dried Beans, pages 5 and 6. Drain beans; discard soak water. In a large saucepan, combine soaked beans, lard or bacon drippings, garlic, 5 cups water and salt. Bring to a boil; reduce heat. Cover and simmer until beans are tender, 1 to 1-1/2 hours. Drain beans. In a medium skillet, break up and brown pork sausage until it loses all pink color. Add onion. Cook and stir 2 minutes. Preheat oven to 350°F (175°C). In a 3-quart casserole, layer half the drained beans, half the cooked sausage mixture and half the sauerkraut, lightly sprinkling each layer with pepper. Repeat layers. Arrange smoky sausage pieces on top of final sauerkraut layer. Pour broth over sausage pieces. Bake uncovered 1 hour. Serve steaming hot. Makes 4 to 6 servings.

If you have assembled a casserole in advance and refrigerated it, let it stand at room temperature 15 to 20 minutes before putting it in the preheated oven. Add 10 minutes to the baking time.

Ham Casserole Amandine

Make this Chinese-style casserole with ham, then try it with cooked chicken, beef or pork.

1 tablespoon butter or margarine
1 tablespoon all-purpose flour
1 cup milk
2 tablespoons soy sauce
1/2 cup dairy sour cream
2 (9-oz.) pkg. frozen French-style
   green beans, thawed

1 (4-oz.) can mushroom pieces, drained
2 cups cubed ham
1 (5-oz.) can water chestnuts, sliced
1-1/2 tablespoons butter or margarine
1 cup fresh fine breadcrumbs, page 102
1/3 cup sliced almonds

In a medium saucepan over low heat, melt 1 tablespoon butter or margarine. Stir in flour to make a smooth paste. Gradually add milk, stirring constantly. Add soy sauce. Stir over medium heat until sauce thickens and comes to a boil. Remove sauce from heat; stir in sour cream. Preheat oven to 350°F (175°C). In a 2-quart casserole, toss together green beans, mushroom pieces, ham and water chestnuts. Pour sauce over mixture. Mix well. In a small skillet over medium-low heat, melt 1-1/2 tablespoons butter or margarine. Add breadcrumbs and almonds. Stir frequently until breadcrumbs are golden brown. Sprinkle breadcrumb mixture over top of casserole. Bake uncovered 30 minutes. Makes 4 to 6 servings.

Deep-Dish Beans & Dumplings

Dumplings won't cook through unless the casserole is hot when you drop in the dough.

1 cup dried red kidney beans
Water for soaking
2-1/2 cups water
1 slice bacon, diced
1 bay leaf
1 teaspoon salt
1 tablespoon vegetable oil
1/2 cup chopped onion
1 garlic clove, minced

1/2 cup diced green pepper
1 (16-oz.) can tomatoes, undrained
1/4 teaspoon black pepper
1 teaspoon dried leaf marjoram
1 medium zucchini, sliced
4 knackwurst or frankfurters,
   cut in 2-inch pieces
1-1/2 cups biscuit mix
1/2 cup water

Sort and soak beans; see How To Prepare Dried Beans, pages 5 and 6. Drain beans; discard soak water. In a medium saucepan, combine soaked beans, 2-1/2 cups water, bacon, bay leaf and salt. Bring to a boil; reduce heat. Cover and simmer until beans are tender, 1 to 1-1/2 hours. In a large skillet, heat oil. Sauté onion, garlic and green pepper until onion is tender but not browned. Add tomatoes, pepper, marjoram, zucchini and knackwurst. Cover and simmer 5 minutes. Preheat oven to 350°F (175°C). In a small bowl, mix together biscuit mix and water. In a 3-quart casserole, combine hot bean mixture and simmered vegetables. Mix well. Drop biscuit dough by spoonfuls on top of hot bean-vegetable mixture. Bake uncovered 30 minutes. Serve generous portions on plates topped with dumplings. Makes 4 to 6 servings.

Thrifty Chicken & Split Peas

Let your budget determine the type of chicken pieces you use.

2 cups yellow split peas
4 cups water
1 garlic clove, minced
1 teaspoon salt
1/2 cup chopped green onions including tops
1 cup sliced fresh mushrooms
2 tablespoons butter or margarine

6 chicken pieces such as thighs, drumsticks, breasts or wings
1 tablespoon vegetable oil
1 (10-3/4-oz.) can cream of chicken soup
1/2 cup chicken broth
1/2 teaspoon dried leaf basil
2 tablespoons chopped fresh parsley

Sort and rinse peas. Bring water to a boil in a medium saucepan. Add peas, garlic and salt. Bring to a boil again and boil 2 minutes. Remove from heat. Cover and let stand 30 minutes. Drain peas; discard liquid. Preheat oven to 350°F (175°C). In a large skillet, sauté green onion and mushrooms in butter or margarine until soft; set aside in a small bowl. In the same skillet, brown chicken in oil. Put peas in a 2-quart casserole with a cover. Spread sautéed green onions and mushrooms over peas. Bury chicken pieces in peas. In a small bowl, combine soup, chicken broth and basil. Stir until smooth. Pour over casserole. Sprinkle top with parsley. Cover and bake 45 minutes. Uncover during the last 10 minutes to lightly brown the top. Makes 6 servings.

How To Make Beef & Biscuit Casserole

1/Roll out biscuit dough to a 12" x 8" rectangle. Spread reserved bean-beef mixture over dough, leaving a 1/2-inch margin. Roll up dough jelly-roll fashion.

2/Turn roll so seam is at the bottom. Cut filled roll into 1-inch slices. Place biscuits on top of hot bean-beef mixture in casserole.

Campfire Supper

Let the campers help themselves from the cooking pot.

1 (32-oz.) can pork and beans in tomato sauce
1 (16-oz.) can sauerkraut, drained

1/2 lb. hot dogs, cut in 1/2-inch slices
1/4 cup Thousand Island dressing, page 69

In a medium saucepan, combine pork and beans, sauerkraut, hot dogs and dressing; stir. Simmer 15 minutes, stirring occasionally. Makes 4 to 6 servings.

Beef & Biscuit Casserole

Biscuits are sure to cook through if they are placed on a hot casserole.

2 cups cooked pinto beans, page 15, or
   1 (15-oz.) can pinto beans
2 cups cooked black-eyed peas, page 15, or
   1 (15-oz.) can black-eyed peas
1/2 lb. ground beef
1/2 cup chopped celery
1/2 cup chopped onion

1/2 cup chopped green pepper
1 garlic clove, minced
1 teaspoon salt
1 teaspoon paprika
1 (6-oz.) can tomato paste
Water
Biscuit Topping, see below

Biscuit Topping:
1-1/2 cups sifted all-purpose flour
2 teaspoons baking powder
1/2 teaspoon salt

1/4 cup shortening
1/2 cup buttermilk or milk
1 cup reserved bean mixture

Prepare pinto beans and black-eyed peas. In a large skillet, brown ground beef until no longer pink. Spoon off all but about 1 tablespoon fat. Push beef to one side. Sauté celery, onion, green pepper and garlic until onion is softened. Stir onion mixture into beef. Add salt and paprika. Drain pinto beans and black-eyed peas, reserving liquid. Add drained beans and peas to beef mixture; mix. Measure reserved bean and pea liquid. Add water to measure 1-1/2 cups. In a small bowl, combine tomato paste and bean liquid mixture. Stir into bean mixture. Remove 1 cup of bean mixture and reserve. Bring remaining bean mixture to a boil. Reduce heat and keep warm. Preheat oven to 350°F (175°C). Prepare Biscuit Topping. Pour hot bean mixture into a 2-quart casserole. Place biscuits on top of bean mixture. Bake uncovered 45 to 50 minutes until biscuits are golden brown. Makes 4 to 6 servings.

Biscuit Topping:
Sift flour, baking powder and salt into a small bowl. Cut in shortening with a pastry blender or 2 knives until dough resembles cornmeal. Stir in buttermilk or milk until just blended. Turn out onto a floured surface and knead lightly 10 times. Roll out to a 12" x 8" rectangle. Spread reserved bean mixture on biscuit dough to within 1/2 inch of edge. Roll up dough, starting from long side. Cut into 1-inch slices.

Curried Chicken & Noodles

Make a fresh fruit salad to go with chicken, green beans and noodles in a curry sauce.

1 (8-oz.) pkg. noodles, uncooked	3/4 teaspoon dried dill weed
6 cups water	1 teaspoon salt
1 tablespoon salt	1/4 teaspoon pepper
1/4 cup all-purpose flour	1 (9-oz.) pkg. frozen French-style
1/2 cup mayonnaise	green beans, thawed
2 cups chicken broth	2 cups diced cooked chicken
1/4 cup white wine	2 tablespoons butter or margarine
1/2 teaspoon curry powder	1 cup fresh fine breadcrumbs, see below

Preheat oven to 350°F (175°C). In a medium saucepan, cook noodles in boiling salted water until tender, about 6 minutes. Drain and set aside. In a small saucepan, blend flour into mayonnaise. Gradually stir in chicken broth. Add wine, curry, dill, salt and pepper. Stir constantly over low heat until mixture thickens. In a 2-1/2-quart casserole, combine cooked noodles, green beans and chicken. Pour sauce over and mix. In a small skillet over medium-low heat, melt butter or margarine. Add breadcrumbs. Stir constantly until breadcrumbs are toasted. Sprinkle toasted breadcrumbs over top of casserole. Bake uncovered 30 minutes. Makes 4 servings.

How To Make Breadcrumbs
For Curried Chicken & Noodles

1/To make fresh fine breadcrumbs, break 2 or 3 slices of bread into 5 or 6 pieces. Process in blender to fine crumbs. Breadcrumbs are ready to use or store. They may be toasted, if desired.

2/To toast breadcrumbs, stir into melted butter or margarine in a skillet. Use about 2 tablespoons butter or margarine to 1 cup of breadcrumbs. Continue stirring breadcrumbs over medium-low heat until golden brown.

Chicken & Limas Paprika

Cook lima beans the day before to make an easy meal on a busy day.

2 cups drained, cooked large lima beans,
   page 15
1/4 cup all-purpose flour
1 teaspoon salt
1 teaspoon paprika
1 (3-lb.) frying chicken, cut in pieces

2 tablespoons vegetable oil
1 medium onion, sliced
1 (9-oz.) pkg. frozen cut green beans, thawed
1 (16-oz.) can tomatoes, undrained, diced
2 teaspoons paprika

Prepare lima beans. Drain and set aside. On a sheet of waxed paper, combine flour, salt and 1 teaspoon paprika. Mix well. Dredge chicken pieces in flour mixture. Heat oil in a large skillet. Brown chicken in hot oil until golden brown. Remove and set aside. Sauté onion in oil remaining in skillet until tender but not browned. Preheat oven to 350°F (175°C). In a shallow 3-1/2-quart casserole, combine onion, lima beans, green beans, tomatoes and 2 teaspoons paprika; mix. Sink chicken pieces into bean mixture. Bake 45 minutes. Serve hot. Makes 4 to 6 servings.

Lamb & Lentils

Next time you go hunting, try this casserole with game meats instead of lamb.

1 tablespoon vegetable oil
4 cross-cut lamb shanks, about 1-lb.
2 garlic cloves, minced
1/2 cup chopped carrot
1/2 cup chopped celery
1 bay leaf
1/2 teaspoon dried leaf thyme
1/2 cup water
1/2 teaspoon salt

Pepper to taste
1 cup dried lentils
1 medium onion, cut in quarters
1 sliver lemon peel
2 cups water
1 teaspoon salt
Fresh parsley, if desired
Lemon peel, if desired

Heat oil in a large skillet with a cover. Brown lamb on both sides in hot oil. Add garlic, carrot, celery, bay leaf, thyme, water, 1/2 teaspoon salt and pepper. Cover and simmer until lamb is tender, about 1 hour. Add more water if necessary during cooking. While lamb is cooking, sort and rinse lentils. In a medium saucepan, combine rinsed lentils, onion, lemon peel, water and 1 teaspoon salt. Bring to a boil; reduce heat. Cover and simmer until lentils are tender, about 45 minutes. Remove onion and lemon peel; discard. Preheat oven to 350°F (175°C). When lamb is tender, remove from skillet and set aside. Stir lentils and cooking liquid into vegetables in skillet. Pour lentil-vegetable mixture into a 2-quart casserole. Top with cooked lamb shanks. Bake uncovered 30 minutes. For each serving, place a piece of lamb on a plate. Surround with lentils. Garnish with a parsley sprig and twist of lemon peel, if desired. Makes 4 servings.

Black Beans With Sausage

Hot Italian sausage makes it extra spicy; use sweet sausage for a milder dish.

2 cups cooked black beans, page 15
1 cup uncooked rice
Water
Salt
1/2 lb. sweet or hot Italian sausage
1/2 cup chopped onion

1/2 cup diced green pepper
1 garlic clove, minced
3 small yellow summer squash
20 cherry tomatoes or 2 medium tomatoes
1/2 teaspoon salt
1/2 teaspoon dried leaf oregano

Prepare beans. Drain, reserving 1/2 cup cooking liquid. Prepare rice with water and salt according to package directions. Remove casings from sausage. In a large skillet, break up sausage and brown over medium heat. Drain on paper towels. Pour all but 2 tablespoons drippings from skillet. Sauté onion, green pepper and garlic in reserved drippings until onion is tender but not browned. Cut squash lengthwise in quarters and then in 1-inch pieces. Peel tomatoes; see page 91. Leave cherry tomatoes whole; coarsely chop medium tomatoes. Add squash pieces, prepared tomatoes, 1/2 teaspoon salt, oregano, beans, reserved cooking liquid and cooked sausage to onion mixture in skillet. Mix well. Cover and simmer 10 minutes. Add rice; toss gently. Makes 4 to 6 servings.

Calico Casserole

Hate to cook? This tasty supper can be assembled in minutes.

1 (10-oz.) pkg. frozen baby lima beans, cooked
2 (16-oz.) cans pork and beans in tomato sauce
1 (15-oz.) can red kidney beans, drained
1/2 lb. frankfurters, cut in 1-inch slices
1 beef bouillon cube
1/2 cup boiling water

1/4 cup ketchup
2 tablespoons brown sugar
1 teaspoon Worcestershire sauce
1 tablespoon prepared mustard
1 (3-oz.) can fried onions

Preheat oven to 350°F (175°C). In a 2-quart casserole, combine lima beans, pork and beans, kidney beans and frankfurters; toss. In a small bowl, dissolve bouillon cube in boiling water. Stir in ketchup, brown sugar, Worcestershire sauce and mustard. Pour mixture over beans; stir. Arrange fried onions over top of bean mixture. Bake 30 minutes. Makes 6 to 8 servings.

Make fresh fine breadcrumbs in your blender and keep them on hand in your freezer. They will keep 4 to 6 weeks. If desired, toast them before using; see page 102.

Beans & Cheese

So much more nutritious than macaroni and cheese—and youngsters love it!

2 cups Savory White Beans made with
   Great Northern Beans,page 18
1 tablespoon butter or margarine
1 tablespoon all-purpose flour
3/4 cup hot milk

2 oz. process American cheese, cut in pieces
1/2 teaspoon salt
1/8 teaspoon white pepper
1/2 cup shredded Cheddar cheese

Prepare Savory White Beans. Drain, reserving 1/4 cup cooking liquid. Preheat oven to 325°F (165°C). In a medium saucepan, melt butter or margarine. Stir in flour. Cook and stir 1 minute until mixture is smooth. Remove from heat. Gradually stir in milk and reserved cooking liquid. Return saucepan to medium heat. Stir constantly until sauce thickens and comes to a boil. Continue to boil 2 minutes, stirring constantly. Add American cheese; stir until cheese melts. Stir in salt and white pepper. Put beans in a 2-quart casserole. Pour cheese mixture over beans. Mix well. Sprinkle shredded Cheddar cheese over top. Bake uncovered 30 minutes. Serve immediately. Makes 3 to 4 servings.

Bean & Sausage Bake

Delicious with a tossed salad and hot corn bread!

2 cups drained, cooked pinto beans,
   page 15, or 1 (15-oz.) can pinto beans,
   drained
1 cup drained, cooked red kidney beans,
   page 15, or 1 (8-oz.) can red kidney beans,
   drained
1 cup drained, cooked garbanzo beans,
   page 15, or 1 (8-oz.) can garbanzo beans,
   drained

1/2 lb. sweet Italian sausage
3/4 cup chopped onion
1/4 cup chopped green pepper
1 (16-oz.) can tomatoes, drained
1 (8-oz.) can tomato sauce
1 teaspoon sugar
1/2 teaspoon dried leaf basil

Prepare beans. Preheat oven to 350°F (175°C). Remove casings from sausage. Brown sausage in a medium skillet. Pour off drippings. Add onion and green pepper to sausage in skillet. Cook, stirring constantly, until onion is softened. In a 2-1/2-quart casserole with a cover, combine beans with sausage mixture. In a small saucepan, combine tomatoes, tomato sauce, sugar and basil. Break up tomatoes with a fork and knife. Bring tomato mixture to a boil; reduce heat. Cover and simmer 5 minutes. Pour tomato mixture over beans and sausage in the casserole; stir. Cover and bake 30 minutes. Makes 4 to 6 servings.

Main Dishes

Add small amounts of meat or poultry to beans for a robust main dish without the cost, fat or cholesterol of a steak or roast beef dinner. Savory Chicken with black-eyed peas will satisfy six hungry appetites and it uses only one 3-pound frying chicken. You can use less expensive cuts of meat because the meat is mainly contributing flavor and nutritional value. Many of these main dishes use inexpensive spicy sausage, ground beef, lamb or ham shanks or chicken.

For other exciting main dishes using beans, see Casseroles, pages 95 to 106, and International Dishes, pages 134 to 147.

Beans can also be the basis for delicious meatless meals. Featuring beans instead of meat as the main attraction can be an adventure in good eating.

When Western Beans combine with rice, cottage cheeese and Cheddar cheese in Spanish Rice & Bean Pie, the result is nutritious and delicious.

FOR VEGETARIANS

Most of the recipes in this book can easily be adapted for a vegetarian diet by omitting meat. You can substitute vegetable stock for meat broth or bouillon. Leaving out meat lowers the quality of the protein. To ensure proper nutritional intake, serve the beans with a dairy or grain product; refer to a nutritional guide of legume and grain complements. See Complementing Proteins, page 3.

Mexican Buffet
Guacamole & Tortilla Chips
Superb Taco Salad, page 62
Mexican-Style Stuffed Peppers,
page 118
Spanish Rice
Almendrado or Fresh Pineapple Slices
Mexican Wedding Cookies

Vegetarian's Delight
Eggplant Rolls, page 132
Brown Rice With Mushroom Pieces
Orange-Bean Salad, page 53
Warm Crusty Rolls
Blueberry Yogurt Pie

Chili Corn-Pone Pie

To save time, use your favorite cornbread mix for the crust.

2 cups drained, cooked black beans or
  red kidney beans, page 15, or
   1 (15-oz.) can red kidney beans, drained
1/2 lb. ground beef
1/3 cup chopped onion
1 cup whole-kernel corn
1 cup drained canned tomatoes, cut up

1 (8-oz.) can tomato sauce
1 teaspoon chili powder
1/2 teaspoon ground cumin
1 teaspoon salt
Corn-Pone Crust, see below
1 cup shredded Cheddar cheese

Corn-Pone Crust:
1-1/2 cups cornmeal
1/2 cup all-purpose flour
1 teaspoon salt
4 teaspoons baking powder

2 eggs
1 cup milk
1/4 cup butter or margarine, melted

Prepare beans. In a large skillet, brown ground beef until no longer pink. Pour off excess fat. Add onion. Cook and stir until onion is softened. Stir in beans, corn, tomatoes, tomato sauce, chili powder, cumin and salt. Preheat oven to 350°F (175°C). Prepare Corn-Pone Crust. Spoon half of the bean filling into each crust. Sprinkle cheese over tops of pies. Bake 45 minutes. Remove from oven. Let stand 5 minutes before cutting into wedges. Makes 8 to 10 servings.

Corn-Pone Crust:

In a medium bowl, combine cornmeal, flour, salt and baking powder. Beat egg in a small bowl. Add milk and melted butter or margarine. Stir to blend. Add egg mixture to cornmeal mixture. Stir until just blended. Grease two 9-inch pie pans. With the back of a spoon, press cornbread batter into each pie pan, forming a crust.

Bowl Of Meatballs

Make breadcrumbs by processing fresh bread in your blender or food processor; see page 102.

1 lb. lean ground beef
4 oz. ground pork
1 cup fresh fine breadcrumbs, page 102
1 egg
1 teaspoon salt
1/4 teaspoon pepper
1/2 teaspoon ground cumin

20 pimiento-stuffed olives
1 (15-oz.) can red kidney beans, drained
1 (15-oz.) can pinto beans, drained
1 (10-1/2-oz.) can beef broth
1 (10-oz.) can enchilada sauce
1 tablespoon cornmeal
Tortilla chips

Preheat oven to 350°F (175°C). In a medium bowl, combine ground beef, ground pork, breadcrumbs, egg, salt, pepper and cumin. Mix well with a fork. For each meatball, shape meat mixture around an olive. Place meatballs on a jelly-roll pan or 12-inch pizza pan. Bake 15 minutes. In a medium saucepan, combine kidney beans, pinto beans, beef broth and enchilada sauce. Bring to a boil, stirring frequently. Add cornmeal, stirring until mixture thickens. Add cooked meatballs. To serve, pour into a serving bowl and garnish with tortilla chips. Makes 4 to 6 servings.

Ham & Sprout Omelet

An omelet pan isn't essential, but it makes the folding and rolling much easier.

Ham & Sprout Filling, see below
3 eggs
1 tablespoon milk

1/8 teaspoon salt
2 teaspoons butter or margarine
1 sprig fresh parsley

Ham & Sprout Filling:
1 teaspoon butter or margarine
1 oz. cubed ham
2 teaspoons chopped chives or green onion

2 teaspoons chopped parsley
1/2 cup mung bean sprouts or lentil sprouts
2 tablespoons cottage cheese or cream cheese

Warm a serving plate. Prepare Ham & Sprout Filling. Beat eggs slightly with a fork. Stir in milk and salt. Heat a 9-inch omelet pan or medium skillet over medium-high heat. Melt butter or margarine in pan. Immediately pour in egg mixture, shaking pan to distribute evenly. Lightly mix with a fork until egg mixture starts to set. Lift up edges so uncooked portion flows underneath. Omelet is done when underneath is solid and center is still moist. Put filling in center of omelet. Raise the handle of pan so omelet slides towards opposite side. With a fork, fold edge of omelet nearest pan over filling. Then with a rolling motion, fold filled portion over. Continue rolling motion so omelet rolls out of pan and onto warmed plate. You should have a filled rolled omelet with 3 folds. Garnish with fresh parsley. Serve immediately. Makes 2 to 4 servings.

Ham & Sprout Filling:

In a small skillet, melt butter or margarine. Add ham, chives or green onion and parsley. Cook and stir 1 minute. Add sprouts. Cook several minutes longer until sprouts begin to soften. Add cottage cheese or cream cheese. Cook until cheese begins to melt.

Variation

Substitute 1/2 cup Texas Chili With Beans, page 86, or Mama's Homemade Chili, page 47, for Ham & Sprout Filling. Fill omelet, reserving about 2 tablespoons chili for garnish. Sprinkle 2 tablespoons shredded Cheddar cheese over filling. Fold filled omelet as directed. Top with reserved chili and 2 tablespoons shredded Cheddar cheese.

Reheat cooked beans over low heat and add a little water as necessary to prevent scorching.

Savory Bean Pizza

Your pizza recipe collection won't be complete until you add this one!

2 cups Savory White Beans made with
   Great Northern beans, page 18
1/4 teaspoon dried leaf oregano
1 tablespoon chopped fresh parsley
Pinch of dried leaf thyme
1/4 teaspoon dried leaf basil
1 cup Pizza Marinara Sauce, page 72
1 pkg. hot roll mix
Water

4 oz. Italian sausage
4 oz. pepperoni, sliced
1 medium onion, sliced, separated in rings
1 tablespoon butter or margarine
1/3 cup sliced ripe olives
1 medium green pepper, cut in rings
2 cups shredded mozzarella cheese
1 cup shredded provolone cheese

Prepare Savory White Beans. Drain, reserving about 1/4 cup cooking liquid. In a medium saucepan, mash beans with a potato masher. Add enough cooking liquid to bring to a spreadable consistency, 2 to 4 tablespoons. Stir in oregano, parsley, thyme and basil. Heat over low heat 10 minutes, stirring frequently. Prepare Pizza Marinara Sauce. Grease a 14-inch pizza pan. Preheat oven to 400°F (205°C). Prepare hot roll mix with water following package directions but omitting egg. Spread dough on pizza pan. Spread bean mixture on dough. Cover with Pizza Marinara Sauce. Remove casing from Italian sausage. In a small skillet, brown sausage. Sprinkle browned sausage over pizza dough. Arrange pepperoni on pizza. In a small skillet, sauté onion rings in butter or margarine until tender but not browned. Arrange onion rings, ripe olives and green pepper rings on top of pizza. Sprinkle with shredded cheeses. Bake 20 to 30 minutes. Makes one 14-inch pizza.

Spanish Rice

Turmeric is sometimes substituted for the more expensive saffron, but the flavor is different.

2 cups drained, cooked garbanzo beans,
   page 15, or 1 (15-oz.) can garbanzo
   beans, drained
2 cups water
2 chicken bouillon cubes
1/4 teaspoon saffron
6 chicken drumsticks
2 tablespoons bacon drippings or vegetable oil

1/2 cup chopped onion
1 garlic clove, minced
1 cup uncooked rice
2 fresh medium tomatoes, peeled, diced
1/2 teaspoon pepper
1/2 teaspoon salt
4 oz. pepperoni, sliced

Prepare garbanzo beans. In a medium saucepan, bring water to a boil. Add bouillon cubes and saffron. Remove from heat; set aside. In a large skillet, brown drumsticks in bacon drippings or oil until golden brown. Remove from skillet and keep warm. Sauté onion and garlic in drippings until onion is softened. Add rice to skillet. Cook until rice is golden, stirring frequently. Add tomatoes, chicken-saffron broth, pepper and salt. Stir in garbanzo beans. Arrange chicken drumsticks like spokes of a wheel on top of rice. Cover and simmer 20 minutes. Arrange pepperoni slices over top. Cover and simmer 10 minutes longer. Serve from the skillet. Makes 4 to 6 servings.

Italian Skillet Dinner

Vegetable oil can be substituted for the olive oil, but it won't give the same flavor.

2 cups drained, cooked Great Northern beans,
    page 15, or 1 (15-oz.) can cannellini
    beans, drained
4 cups water
1 teaspoon salt
1 cup small shell or elbow macaroni
1/2 cup chopped onion
2 garlic cloves, minced

2 tablespoons olive oil
1 large tomato, peeled, chopped
1 (8-oz.) can tomato sauce
1 tablespoon chopped fresh parsley
Pinch of dried leaf basil
1/2 teaspoon dried leaf oregano
Pepper to taste
4 slices provolone cheese

Prepare beans; set aside. In a medium saucepan, bring water and salt to a boil. Add macaroni. Cook until macaroni is just tender, about 8 minutes, stirring occasionally. Drain; set aside. In a large skillet, sauté onion and garlic in olive oil until onion is tender but not browned. Stir in tomato, tomato sauce, parsley, basil, oregano and pepper. Cover and simmer 5 minutes. Add beans and macaroni to sauce; mix well. Arrange cheese slices over mixture. Cover and simmer over very low heat 15 minutes. Serve from the skillet with a spatula. Makes 4 servings.

Braised Short Ribs & Beans

On a cold winter evening, these beans will remind you of a backyard barbecue.

4 lbs. beef short ribs
2 teaspoons salt
1/2 teaspoon pepper
1/2 teaspoon dried leaf oregano
1/2 teaspoon dried leaf basil
2 tablespoons chili powder

2 to 4 tablespoons vegetable oil
1 large onion, sliced
2 garlic cloves, minced
2 cups red wine
2 (15-oz.) cans dark red kidney beans, drained

Preheat oven to 350°F (175°C). Trim excess fat from ribs. In a small bowl, combine salt, pepper, oregano, basil and chili powder. Mix well. Rub seasonings into ribs, covering all sides. Heat 2 tablespoons oil in a medium skillet. Brown ribs in oil until golden brown on all sides. Remove ribs and set aside. Add remaining oil if needed. Sauté onion and garlic in oil until onion softens. Cover bottom of a shallow 4-quart casserole with sautéed onion mixture. Place ribs on top of onion. Pour in wine. Cover and bake until ribs are fork tender, 1-1/2 to 2 hours. Add beans. Cover and bake 30 minutes longer. Remove ribs and place on a warmed platter. Stir beans into pan juices before spooning around ribs. Makes 6 to 8 servings.

Spanish Rice & Bean Pie

Refrigerate the remaining beaten egg and use it in scrambled eggs tomorrow.

2 cups cooked Western Beans, page 17
1 teaspoon ground cumin
1 cup water
1 chicken bouillon cube
1/2 cup uncooked rice
1/2 cup chopped onion

1/2 cup chopped green pepper
1 tablespoon butter or margarine
2 tablespoons chopped pimiento
2 tablespoons beaten egg
1 cup cottage cheese
1/2 cup shredded Cheddar cheese

Prepare Western Beans. Drain, reserving 1/4 cup cooking liquid. Return reserved liquid to beans. Stir in cumin; set beans aside. In a small saucepan, bring water and bouillon cube to a boil. Stir to dissolve bouillon. Add rice to bouillon. Bring to a boil. Reduce heat to lowest setting. Cover and simmer 20 minutes. Preheat oven to 325°F (135°C). In a small skillet, sauté onion and green pepper in butter or margarine until onion is tender but not browned. Stir in pimiento. Add onion mixture and egg to cooked rice; mix well. Oil a 9-inch pie pan. Press rice mixture into pie pan to form a crust. Spread cottage cheese over rice crust. Pour beans over cottage cheese. Bake 20 minutes. Sprinkle top with Cheddar cheese and bake another 20 minutes. Remove from oven; let stand 10 minutes before cutting in wedges. Serve with a spatula. Makes 4 to 6 servings.

How To Make Spanish Rice & Bean Pie

1/Using the back of a spoon, spread rice and green pepper mixture over the bottom and around the sides of an oiled pie pan.

2/Spread cottage cheese over bottom of rice crust and partially up the sides. Pour Western Beans into the cheese-lined crust and bake.

Dixie Platter

Loaded with protein and flavor.

3 cups drained, cooked black-eyed peas, page 15, or 2 (15-oz.) cans black-eyed peas, drained
1 cup uncooked rice
Water
Salt
2 tablespoons butter or margarine
1/4 cup finely chopped onion
1 garlic clove, minced

1 tablespoon all-purpose flour
1/2 teaspoon salt
1/8 teaspoon pepper
1 cup milk
3/4 cup shredded Monterey Jack cheese
1/4 cup freshly grated Parmesan cheese
4 oz. pork sausage
Tomato slices, if desired
Green pepper rings, if desired

Prepare black-eyed peas. Prepare rice with water and salt according to package directions. In a medium saucepan, melt butter or margarine. Sauté onion and garlic in saucepan until onion is tender but not browned. Stir in flour, salt and pepper to make a paste. Gradually add milk, stirring constantly. Bring to a boil, still stirring constantly. Add Monterey Jack and Parmesan cheeses. Stir until cheeses are completely melted; set aside. In a large skillet, brown pork sausage until no longer pink. Spoon off excess fat. Add black-eyed peas to sausage; stir. Pour cheese sauce over sausage and peas; mix. Turn rice onto a platter. Make a well in the center. Pour sausage mixture into well in rice. If desired, garnish with overlapping slices of tomato and green pepper rings. Makes 4 servings.

Curried Chicken & Limas

Serve with rice and condiments of chopped almonds or cashews, lime wedges and chutney.

4 cups Savory White Beans made with large lima beans, page 18
1 (10-3/4-oz.) can chicken broth
1 tablespoon vegetable oil
2 chicken breasts, skinned, boned, page 117
1 medium onion, chopped
1 garlic clove, minced

3 medium carrots, sliced
1/2 medium green pepper, diced
2 teaspoons curry powder
2 tablespoons butter or margarine
2 tablespoons all-purpose flour
1 teaspoon salt

Prepare Savory White Beans; drain. Reserve cooking liquid. Add chicken broth to liquid to make 1-1/2 cups; set aside. Reserve remaining chicken broth. Flatten boneless chicken breasts. With your fingers, separate the small muscle on underside of each breast. Cut each breast in half lengthwise. Roll up each piece, starting at the short side; secure with a wooden pick. Heat oil in a medium skillet. Brown chicken rolls. Add remaining reserved chicken broth. Reduce heat. Cover and simmer until chicken is tender, about 20 minutes. Remove wooden picks. Preheat oven to 350°F (175°C). Sauté onion, garlic, carrot, green pepper and curry powder in butter or margarine until onion is tender but not browned. Stir in flour and salt. Gradually stir in reserved cooking liquid and broth mixture. Stir constantly over medium heat until thickened. Combine beans and curry sauce in a 3-quart casserole. Sink rolled chicken breasts in curried beans. Cover and bake 30 minutes. Serve a chicken roll on each plate surrounded by curried limas. Makes 4 servings.

Savory Chicken

Delicious with buttermilk biscuits and Wilted Green Salad, page 66.

2 cups dried black-eyed peas	2 garlic cloves, minced
5 cups water	1 teaspoon salt
3 chicken bouillon cubes	1 teaspoon ground ginger
1 (2-inch) sliver lemon peel	1/4 teaspoon ground cumin
3/4 cup finely chopped onion	1/4 teaspoon turmeric
1 carrot, grated	2 drops Tabasco sauce
1 teaspoon salt	1 (3-lb.) frying chicken, cut in pieces
1 cup plain yogurt	2 tablespoons vegetable oil
3 tablespoons lemon juice	

Sort and rinse black-eyed peas. Bring 5 cups water to a boil in a large saucepan. Add bouillon cubes; stir to dissolve. Add rinsed peas, lemon peel, onion, carrot and 1 teaspoon salt. Bring to a boil; reduce heat. Cover and simmer until peas are tender, 1 to 1-1/2 hours. In a 9-inch square baking pan, combine yogurt, lemon juice, garlic, 1 teaspoon salt, ginger, cumin, turmeric and Tabasco sauce. Stir well. Add chicken pieces to yogurt mixture, turning to coat on all sides. Set aside to marinate while peas are cooking. Drain peas, reserving 1/2 cup cooking liquid. Remove and discard lemon peel. Preheat oven to 350°F (175°C). In a large skillet, heat oil. Remove chicken pieces from marinade. Brown in skillet until golden on all sides. In a 2-1/2-quart casserole with a cover, combine peas, remaining marinade and reserved cooking liquid. Stir well. Place chicken pieces on top of peas. Cover and bake 45 minutes. To serve, place pieces of chicken in individual gratin dishes or rimmed plates. Surround with black-eyed peas and sauce. Makes 6 servings.

Hoppin' John

Put a bottle of hot pepper sauce on the table for those who like it extra spicy.

1-1/2 cups dried black-eyed peas	1/4 teaspoon black pepper
4 cups water	Dash of cayenne pepper
3 slices bacon	1 cup chopped onion
1 garlic clove, minced	1 cup water
1 bay leaf	1/2 cup rice
1/2 teaspoon dried leaf marjoram	1/2 teaspoon salt
3/4 teaspoon salt	

Sort and rinse peas. Put peas and 4 cups water in a medium saucepan. In a medium skillet, fry bacon until crisp. Drain on paper towels. Reserve bacon drippings. Add 1 tablespoon drippings, garlic, bay leaf, marjoram, 3/4 teaspoon salt, black pepper and cayenne pepper to peas; stir. Bring to a boil; reduce heat. Cover and simmer until tender, 1 to 1-1/2 hours. In another medium saucepan, sauté onion in 1 tablespoon reserved bacon drippings until onion is tender but not browned. Add 1 cup water. Bring to a boil. Add rice and 1/2 teaspoon salt. Reduce heat to lowest setting and simmer 20 minutes. Drain peas and discard bay leaf. Toss peas with hot, cooked rice. Turn into a serving dish and sprinkle with crumbled bacon. Makes 3 or 4 servings.

Ginger Steak

If you don't have fresh ginger root, substitute 1/4 teaspoon ground ginger.

1-1/2 lbs. round steak	1 cup sliced celery
2 tablespoons all-purpose flour	1 small onion, sliced
1 tablespoon vegetable oil	1/2 medium green pepper
1 tablespoon shredded fresh ginger root	2 cups fresh mung bean sprouts or
1-1/2 cups water	1 (16-oz.) can bean sprouts, drained
1 beef bouillon cube	1 tablespoon cornstarch
2 tablespoons soy sauce	1 (10-1/2-oz.) can beef broth

On a sheet of waxed paper, dredge steak with flour. Pound both sides with a meat mallet to tenderize. In a large skillet, brown steak in oil on both sides. Add ginger root, water, bouillon cube and soy sauce. Cover and simmer until meat is tender, about 1 hour. Place meat on a platter; keep warm. Add celery, onion, green pepper and bean sprouts to skillet. Cover and cook 10 minutes. Remove vegetables from skillet with a slotted spoon. Cover steak with vegetables; keep warm. Combine cornstarch and broth in a small bowl. Stir into liquid remaining in skillet. Bring to a boil, stirring constantly. Pour sauce over vegetables and meat. Makes 4 servings.

Chuckwagon Pot Roast

Tryed it once, that's enough. 10-9-97

Served with hot biscuits, this Western round-up meal will fill the hungriest ranch hands.

3 lbs. bottom round roast or chuck roast	2 cups water
2 teaspoons salt	2 tablespoons vegetable oil
1/4 teaspoon pepper	1 garlic clove, minced
1/2 teaspoon paprika	1/2 cup chopped onion
1/2 cup dried large lima beans	1 (10-1/2-oz.) can beef broth (1-1/4 cups)
1/2 cup dried baby lima beans	1/2 cup chili sauce
1/2 cup dried pinto beans	3 carrots, cut in 1-inch pieces
Water for soaking	

Rub roast with salt, pepper and paprika. Refrigerate several hours or overnight. Sort and soak beans; see How To Prepare Dried Beans, pages 5 and 6. Drain beans; discard soak water. In a 4-quart pot, combine soaked beans and 2 cups water. In a large skillet, brown roast in oil to a deep brown. Place roast on top of beans. Sauté garlic and onion in drippings in skillet until onion is softened. Stir in beef broth and chili sauce. Cook and stir 2 to 3 minutes, scraping browned bits from skillet. Pour sauce over pot roast. Bring to a boil; reduce heat. Cover and simmer until meat and beans are almost tender, about 2 hours. Add carrots. Cover and simmer 30 minutes longer. Place meat on a platter. Surround with beans and carrots. Makes 6 to 8 servings.

Chicken Chow Mein

Stir-fry *means to stir and toss rapidly in oil over high heat.*

1 tablespoon soy sauce

2 tablespoons cornstarch

2 tablespoons dry white wine or water

2 chicken breasts

1 cup water

1 chicken bouillon cube

3 cups fresh mung bean sprouts or
    1 (16-oz.) can bean sprouts

2 tablespoons vegetable oil

2 celery ribs, sliced diagonally

1 small onion, cut in half lengthwise and sliced

4 oz. fresh mushrooms, sliced, or
    1 (4-oz.) can mushrooms, drained

1/2 teaspoon salt

1 (3-oz.) can Chow Mein noodles or
    2 cups cooked rice

In a small bowl, combine soy sauce, cornstarch and wine or water. Remove skin from chicken breasts. Remove bone and cut chicken in 1/4" x 2" slivers. Stir chicken into soy sauce marinade and set aside. Heat water in a small saucepan. Add bouillon cube; stir to dissolve. Cool. Wash and drain fresh bean sprouts in a colander or drain canned sprouts. Heat oil in a wok or large skillet over medium-high heat. Lift chicken slivers from marinade and put in wok. Stir-fry 5 minutes or until chicken turns white. Stir in celery and onion. Stir-fry 3 minutes. Add mushrooms. Stir-fry 2 minutes. Add bean sprouts, chicken broth, remaining marinade and salt. Cook and stir until sprouts soften slightly, about 2 minutes. Serve over rice or Chow Mein noodles. Makes 2 to 4 servings.

How To Remove Skin & Bones From Chicken
For Chicken Chow Mein

1/To remove skin from chicken breasts, lift skin and, with a sharp knife, cut membranes attaching skin to meat. The skin will pull away easily.

2/Hold breast with wing edge on cutting board. Run a knife lengthwise along bone. Lift meat away from bone and repeat, going deeper into the breast along the bone. Cut meat away from the wishbone, back and wing.

Italian-Style Stuffed Peppers

Green peppers, high in Vitamin C, are natural and nutritious containers for serving.

1/3 cup Italian Salad Dressing, page 66	1 garlic clove, minced
4 medium green peppers	1/3 cup chopped onion
1 qt. water	2 teaspoons butter or margarine
1/2 teaspoon salt	2 cups drained, cooked red kidney beans,
1-1/2 cups water	page 15, or 1 (15-oz.) can red kidney
3/4 teaspoon salt	beans, drained
3/4 cup uncooked rice	2 tablespoons chopped fresh parsley
1 (15-oz.) can tomato sauce	1 (4-oz.) pkg. sliced provolone cheese,
1 teaspoon salt	cut in strips
1/2 teaspoon dried leaf basil	

Prepare Italian Salad Dressing. Wash peppers. Cut a 1/2-inch slice off top of each pepper, removing stem. Wash inside peppers and remove seeds. In a large saucepan, bring 1 quart water and 1/2 teaspoon salt to a boil. Add peppers; boil 3 minutes. Drain peppers upside down on paper towels. In a medium saucepan, bring 1-1/2 cups water and 3/4 teaspoon salt to a boil. Stir in rice. Reduce heat to lowest setting. Cover and simmer 20 minutes until tender. In a small saucepan, combine tomato sauce, 1 teaspoon salt, basil and garlic. Cover and simmer 10 minutes. In a medium skillet, sauté onion in butter or margarine until tender but not browned. Add beans and parsley. Mix well. Add cooked rice to bean mixture. Stir in salad dressing. Place peppers in an 8-inch square baking pan. Fill each pepper with rice-bean mixture. Pour sauce over filled peppers. Bake uncovered 30 minutes. Place cheese strips over top of each pepper. Bake 10 minutes longer. Makes 4 servings.

Tamale-Stuffed Peppers

Crush tortilla chips between sheets of waxed paper with a rolling pin.

2 cups Chili Beans, page 19, or	1 (16-oz.) can tamales
1 (16-oz.) can chili beans	1/3 cup chopped onion
4 medium green peppers	1 cup shredded Cheddar cheese
3 qts. water	1 cup crushed tortilla chips
1 tablespoon salt	

Prepare Chili Beans. Cut peppers in half lengthwise. Wash and remove stems, seeds and membranes. In a 4-quart pot, cook peppers in boiling salted water 3 minutes. Drain upside down on paper towels. Drain tamales, reserving sauce; remove paper. Cut tamales into bite-size pieces. In a large saucepan, combine tamale pieces, reserved tamale sauce and beans. Stir in chopped onion. Cover and cook over low heat 15 minutes. Stir in 1/2 cup cheese. Preheat oven to 350°F (175°C). Fill peppers with bean-tamale mixture. Place stuffed peppers in a 13" x 9" baking pan. Pour water about 1/8 inch deep into pan. Bake 20 minutes. Top each pepper with crushed tortilla chips and remaining cheese. Bake 5 to 7 minutes longer until cheese begins to melt. Makes 6 to 8 servings.

Vegetables

Fresh green beans and peas are featured in this section as well as combinations of fresh vegetables and cooked dried beans.

When buying fresh green beans, look for crisp, bright pods with no serious blemishes. Young tender beans should snap when folded end to end. Old beans have thick, tough and often wilted or flabby pods. Store fresh beans in a vegetable crisper or plastic bag in the refrigerator. They are best eaten the same day they are picked, but will retain their fresh flavor for 2 or 3 days.

When buying fresh peas, choose firm pods that are visibly filled with peas. *Snow peas*, also called *China peas* and *pea pods*, should be crisp but flat with the peas barely perceptible to your touch. Fresh peas can be refrigerated 3 to 5 days.

Fresh lima beans are not generally available, but if you are able to find them, look for firm, bright beans. Store them in the refrigerator, but not longer than 3 to 5 days.

Canned beans lack the brightness, full flavor and crispness of fresh or frozen beans. But they are very satisfying in casseroles, such as Honey-Lemon Beans, or served in a sauce, such as in Devilish Beans.

Combining fresh vegetables and cooked dried beans will give you delicious nutritious dishes. It's also an economical way to use leftover cooked dried beans. Dark red kidney beans add color and an unusual flavor to Confetti Beans. Fresh spinach is a delight when cooked with pinto beans, bacon and cream to make Fresh Spinach & Beans. Pinto beans seem a natural addition to Mexicali Vegetables.

Eggplant Rolls and Stuffed Zucchini—one filled with garbanzo beans, the other with soybeans—can be served as meatless main dishes. You don't have to be a vegetarian to enjoy them.

Party Buffet
Shrimp & Bean Cocktail, page 60
Melba Toast
Roast Beef Au Jus
Celery-Cheese Casserole, page 123
Mushroom & Spinach Salad
Poppy Seed Rolls
Pound Cake Topped With
Fresh Fruit & Custard Sauce

Winter Barbecue
Braised Short Ribs & Beans, page 112
Cottage Fried Potatoes
Zesty Green Beans, page 130
Sprout Slaw, page 56
Peach Upside-Down Cake

Stuffed Zucchini

Toast seeds in a heavy skillet over medium-high heat until golden, 3 to 5 minutes.

1 cup dried soybeans
Water for soaking
3 cups water
1 tablespoon vegetable oil
1 teaspoon salt
1-1/2 cups cooked brown rice
3 green onions, sliced
1/4 cup chopped fresh parsley
1/4 teaspoon pepper

1 cup water
1 teaspoon salt
4 medium zucchini (about 6 inches long)
2 tablespoons butter or margarine
1 cup fresh fine breadcrumbs, page 102
1/4 cup toasted sesame seeds or
    hulled sunflower seeds
4 slices process American cheese

Sort and soak soybeans; see how to Prepare Dried Beans, pages 5 and 6. Drain soybeans; discard soak water. In a medium saucepan, combine soaked beans, 3 cups water, oil and 1 teaspoon salt. Bring to a boil; reduce heat. Cover and simmer 3 hours. Add water if necessary during cooking to keep beans just covered. Cooked beans will still be quite firm. Prepare rice. Drain soybeans, reserving 1/2 cup cooking liquid. Coarsely mash soybeans with a potato masher, adding reserved cooking liquid. In a medium bowl. combine mashed soybeans, rice, green onions, parsley and pepper. Preheat oven to 350°F (175°C). In a medium saucepan, bring 1 cup water with 1 teaspoon salt to a boil. Add zucchini. Cook 5 minutes. Drain zucchini on paper towels. Cut each zucchini in half lengthwise. Scoop out centers, leaving a 1/4-inch shell. Chop zucchini centers and add to beans and rice. Arrange zucchini shells in a 13" x 9" baking pan. Fill shells with soybean mixture. In a small skillet, melt butter or margarine. Add breadcrumbs. Stir constantly over medium heat until breadcrumbs brown. Add seeds. Stir 1 to 2 minutes longer. Sprinkle breadcrumb mixture over stuffed zucchini. Cut each cheese slice in half diagonally. Place 1 cheese triangle on each stuffed zucchini half. Bake uncovered 30 minutes. Makes 4 to 6 servings.

Devilish Green Beans

Green beans in a tangy cream sauce go well with almost everything.

2 (16-oz.) cans cut green beans, undrained
1/2 cup chopped onion
1/2 cup chopped green pepper
2 tablespoons butter or margarine
2 teaspoons all-purpose flour
1 teaspoon salt

1/8 teaspoon black pepper
1 tablespoon prepared mustard
2 egg yolks, beaten
1 cup milk, warmed
2 tablespoons lemon juice

In a medium saucepan, heat green beans 10 minutes. Drain and keep warm. In a medium skillet, sauté onion and green pepper in butter or margarine until onion is tender but not browned. Remove from heat. Sprinkle flour, salt and black pepper over onion mixture. Stir until smooth. Stir in mustard and egg yolks. Slowly stir in milk. Stir over low heat until mixture is smooth and thickened. Stir in lemon juice. Pour over beans; toss. Cover and simmer 5 minutes. Makes 4 to 6 servings.

Vegetable Stir-Fry

Before you begin to stir-fry, have all the ingredients ready and within easy reach.

1 lb. fresh green beans or	1 teaspoon sugar
2 (9-oz.) pkgs. frozen cut green beans	1 (6-oz.) can water chestnuts, drained, sliced
2 tablespoons vegetable oil	1/2 cup chicken broth
1 cup diagonally sliced celery	1 tablespoon cornstarch
3 green onions, cut in 1/2-inch pieces	2 tablespoons water
1-1/2 teaspoons salt	1/4 cup sliced almonds

Snap off ends of fresh beans and cut into 2-inch pieces. Frozen green beans should be partially thawed. Heat a wok or large heavy skillet over high heat 30 seconds. Add oil; heat 30 seconds longer. Reduce heat to medium. Combine green beans, celery and green onions in wok and stir-fry 2 minutes. Add salt, sugar, water chestnuts and chicken broth. Stir-fry 1 minute. Cover and cook 10 minutes. While vegetables are cooking, dissolve cornstarch in water. Add to vegetables. Stir constantly over medium heat until beans are coated with a thin glaze. Turn into a serving dish and sprinkle with almonds. Serve hot. Makes 4 to 6 servings.

Pilgrim Pudding

As elegant as a soufflé, but it won't puff as high.

1/4 cup butter or margarine	1-1/4 cups milk, warmed
1/4 cup all-purpose flour	1 (16-oz.) can cream-style corn
1-1/2 teaspoons salt	3 eggs, separated
1 tablespoon sugar	1 (10-oz.) pkg. frozen baby lima beans, cooked

Preheat oven to 350°F (175°C). Butter a 2-quart soufflé dish. In a medium saucepan, melt 1/4 cup butter or margarine. Stir in flour, salt and sugar. Cook until bubbly. Gradually add milk, stirring constantly. Stir in corn. Cook until mixture is thickened and bubbly. Remove from heat. In a small bowl, slightly beat egg yolks. Gradually add about 1/2 cup thickened corn mixture to egg yolks, stirring constantly. Stir egg yolk mixture into corn mixture in saucepan. Stir in lima beans. In a small bowl, beat egg whites until stiff but not dry. Fold beaten egg whites into corn and lima bean mixture. Pour into buttered soufflé dish. Bake 1 hour. Serve immediately. Makes 4 to 6 servings.

One 16-ounce can of bean sprouts equals two cups of fresh mung bean sprouts.

Green Beans Amandine

Try other nuts, too—such as hazelnuts or Brazil nuts!

1/2 cup slivered almonds	1/4 cup dry onion soup mix
1-1/2 lbs. fresh green beans	1 teaspoon cornstarch
1 cup water	1 tablespoon cold water

In a small skillet over medium heat, stir almonds until they are golden. Set aside. Break tips off green beans; wash beans. Combine 1 cup water and soup mix in a large skillet. Bring to a boil, stirring to dissolve soup mix. Add beans; reduce heat. Cover and simmer 10 to 15 minutes until beans are crisp-tender. Drain, reserving cooking liquid in a small saucepan. Set beans aside. Dissolve cornstarch in 1 tablespoon cold water. Add to reserved cooking liquid. Stir over medium-high heat until mixture becomes thickened and clear. Pour sauce over beans in skillet; toss. Heat 3 to 5 minutes. Sprinkle toasted almonds over beans and toss again. Makes 4 to 6 servings.

Green Beans With Blue Cheese

Quick and elegant.

1/2 cup water	1/8 teaspoon pepper
1/2 teaspoon salt	2 tablespoons crumbled blue cheese
1 (9-oz.) pkg. frozen French-style green beans	1/2 cup fresh fine breadcrumbs, page 102
1 tablespoon butter or margarine	1/2 tablespoon butter or margarine

Preheat oven to 350°F (175°C). In a medium saucepan, bring water and salt to a boil. Add green beans. Bring water to a boil again. Reduce heat. Cover and simmer until beans are tender, about 10 minutes; drain. Toss cooked beans with 1 tablespoon butter or margarine, pepper and blue cheese. In a small skillet, toast breadcrumbs in 1/2 tablespoon butter or margarine until golden brown, stirring constantly. Turn beans into a small casserole and sprinkle with toasted breadcrumbs. Bake uncovered 15 minutes. Makes 3 to 4 servings.

Celery-Cheese Casserole

This casserole is easy to prepare and elegant enough for a formal dinner.

1 cup diagonally sliced celery	1 (10-oz.) pkg. frozen chopped broccoli, thawed
1/2 tablespoon butter or margarine	
1 (9-oz.) pkg. frozen green beans, thawed	1 (10-1/2-oz.) can cream of celery soup
1 (10-oz.) pkg. frozen cut asparagus, thawed	1 cup shredded American cheese

Preheat oven to 350°F (175°C). In a small skillet, sauté celery in butter or margarine until softened but not browned. In a 2-quart casserole, combine sautéed celery, green beans, asparagus and broccoli. Stir in soup. Cover and bake 40 minutes. Uncover and sprinkle with cheese. Bake uncovered 15 minutes. Serve hot. Makes 6 to 8 servings.

Broccoli & Chick Peas

Chick peas are also known as garbanzo beans.

2 cups drained, cooked garbanzo beans,
   page 15, or 1 (15-oz.) can garbanzo
   beans, drained
3/4 lb. fresh broccoli or 1 (10-oz.)
   pkg. frozen broccoli spears, thawed
1/2 cup water
1/2 teaspoon salt

2 tablespoons chopped canned pimiento
1 (6-oz.) jar marinated artichoke hearts,
   undrained
1 teaspoon lemon juice
1/2 teaspoon dried leaf basil
1/4 teaspoon salt
Pepper to taste

Prepare garbanzo beans; drain. Wash and trim fresh broccoli. Cut fresh or frozen broccoli into 1-inch pieces. In a medium saucepan, bring water and salt to a boil. Add broccoli. Bring to a boil again; reduce heat. Cover and simmer until broccoli is tender, 10 to 12 minutes for fresh broccoli or 5 to 7 minutes for thawed frozen broccoli; drain. Add garbanzo beans, pimiento, artichoke hearts, lemon juice, basil, salt and pepper to drained broccoli in saucepan. Toss gently. Cook until heated through, about 10 minutes. Turn into a serving dish. Serve hot. Makes 4 to 6 servings.

Snow Peas & Sprouts

Marvelous with hamburgers, pork chops or chicken!

2 cups mung bean sprouts or lentil sprouts
1/2 cup beef broth
1 tablespoon soy sauce
1 tablespoon cornstarch
4 slices bacon
2 celery ribs, sliced diagonally

1/2 medium onion, sliced
4 oz. fresh mushrooms, sliced or
   1 (4-oz.) can mushrooms
1 cup fresh snow peas or
   1 (6-oz.) pkg. frozen snow peas

Wash and drain sprouts in a colander. In a small bowl, combine beef broth, soy sauce and cornstarch. In a wok or large skillet, fry bacon until crisp. Drain on paper towels. Spoon off all but 2 table-spoons bacon drippings. Sauté celery and onion in wok until onion is tender but not browned. Add mushrooms and snow peas. Stir-fry 3 minutes. Add drained sprouts; stir. Pour beef broth mixture over vegetables. Stir over medium heat 2 minutes. Turn vegetables into a serving bowl. Crumble bacon and sprinkle over casserole. Makes 4 servings.

Variation

Add 1/2 pound of drained tofu, cut into 1/4-inch cubes. Add to celery and onion with mushrooms and snow peas.

Curried Limas

Try this with frozen green beans, too.

1 cup water
1 teaspoon salt
2 (10-oz.) pkgs. frozen baby lima beans
2 slices bacon, diced
1/4 cup chopped onion

1 teaspoon curry powder
1 (10-3/4-oz.) can cream of mushroom soup
2 tablespoons maple syrup or
    maple-flavored syrup
1/2 cup chili sauce

In a medium saucepan, bring water with salt to a boil. Add lima beans. Cook until just tender, about 15 minutes. Drain, reserving cooking liquid. In a medium skillet, fry bacon until crisp. Drain on paper towels. Pour off bacon drippings, leaving 1 tablespoon drippings in skillet. Sauté onion in remaining drippings until softened. Stir in curry powder. Add soup, syrup, chili sauce and reserved cooking liquid. Mix well. Bring to a boil. Stir in lima beans. Cover and simmer 20 minutes. Stir in bacon. Simmer 5 minutes. Makes 4 to 6 servings.

Fresh Spinach & Beans

Wash spinach thoroughly by immersing it in a large bowl of cold water.

1 cup drained, cooked pinto beans, page 15,
    or 1/2 (15-oz.) can pinto beans, drained
1 lb. fresh spinach
2 slices bacon

1/2 teaspoon salt
Pepper to taste
2 tablespoons light cream or half-and-half

Prepare pinto beans. Wash spinach and remove stems. Drain spinach on paper towels, then chop finely. In a large skillet, fry bacon until crisp. Drain on paper towels. Toss beans in bacon drippings in skillet. Cover and simmer 10 minutes. Add spinach. Sprinkle with salt and pepper; toss. Cover and simmer 5 minutes. Add cream. Simmer 2 minutes, stirring frequently. Do not boil. Crumble bacon over mixture; stir. Makes 3 to 4 servings.

Confetti Beans

Try this quick and easy way to brighten a routine meal.

1 (15-oz.) can cut green beans, undrained
1 (15-oz.) can cut wax beans, drained
1 (8-oz.) can red kidney beans, drained
1 teaspoon Worcestershire sauce

1/4 teaspoon pepper
1/2 teaspoon dry mustard
1 (3-oz.) pkg. cream cheese, cut in small cubes

In a medium saucepan, combine undrained green beans, drained wax beans and drained red kidney beans. Cover and cook 15 minutes over medium heat. Drain and return to saucepan. Stir in Worcestershire sauce, pepper, mustard and cream cheese. Stir constantly over medium heat until cheese melts. Turn into a serving dish. Makes 4 to 6 servings.

Mexicali Vegetables

Grated carrot and diagonally sliced celery cook faster than plain-sliced vegetables.

2 cups drained, cooked pinto beans,
    page 15, or 1 (15-oz.) can pinto beans,
    drained
1 lb. fresh green beans or
    2 (9-oz.) pkgs. frozen cut green beans
1/4 cup butter or margarine
1 garlic clove, minced

1 cup grated carrot
1 cup chopped onion
1 cup diagonally sliced celery
1/3 cup Green Chili Salsa, page 69, or
    canned green chili salsa
1 tablespoon prepared mustard

Prepare pinto beans. Break ends off fresh green beans. Cut green beans into 1-inch pieces. Melt butter or margarine in a large skillet over medium heat. Add garlic. Cook and stir 1 minute. Add cut green beans, carrot, onion and celery to onion mixture. Toss to mix and coat vegetables. Cover and cook 5 minutes. Combine salsa and mustard. Stir into vegetable mixture. Add pinto beans; toss. Cook uncovered until heated through, about 10 minutes. Makes 6 to 8 servings.

Fresh Vegetable Bake

Enjoy this after a hard day's work in your garden.

1 cup fresh green beans, washed,
    cut in 1-inch slices
2 carrots, thinly sliced
1/2 cup sliced celery
1/2 medium cauliflower,
    separated into flowerets
1/2 green or red sweet pepper, seeded,
    cut in thin strips
1 zucchini, thinly sliced
1 yellow summer squash, thinly sliced
1/2 cup fresh shelled green peas

1 medium onion, sliced
2 medium tomatoes, peeled, cut in wedges
1/2 cup beef broth
2 tablespoons olive oil
2 garlic cloves, minced
1 teaspoon salt
1 bay leaf
1 teaspoon dried dill weed
1/2 cup freshly grated Parmesan cheese,
    if desired

Preheat oven to 350°F (175°C). Layer vegetables in a 4-quart casserole with a cover. In a small saucepan, combine broth, oil, garlic, salt, bay leaf and dill weed. Bring to a boil and pour over vegetables. Cover casserole and bake 1 hour. Remove and discard bay leaf. If desired, sprinkle with Parmesan cheese before serving. Makes 6 to 8 servings.

Creamy Creole Limas

Especially good with meat loaf or pork chops.

1/2 cup water	1 (8-oz.) can tomato sauce
1/2 teaspoon salt	1 medium tomato, peeled, diced
1 (10-oz.) pkg. frozen lima beans	1/2 teaspoon salt
1/3 cup chopped onion	1/4 teaspoon black pepper
1/2 cup chopped green pepper	1/2 teaspoon sugar
1 tablespoon butter or margarine	1 (3-oz.) pkg. cream cheese, cut in small cubes

In a medium saucepan, bring water and 1/2 teaspoon salt to a boil. Add lima beans. Cook until tender, about 15 minutes. Drain and set aside. In a medium saucepan, sauté onion and green pepper in butter or margarine until onion is tender but not browned. Add tomato sauce, tomato, 1/2 teaspoon salt, black pepper and sugar. Stir well. Cover and simmer 10 minutes. Stir in cooked lima beans and cream cheese. Simmer until thoroughly heated and cheese is melted, about 5 minutes. Makes 3 to 4 servings.

Cheese Soufflé

Sprinkle the buttered soufflé dish with fine breadcrumbs so the soufflé won't stick.

3 tablespoons butter or margarine	1/2 cup chicken broth
2 tablespoons finely chopped onion	1/2 cup milk
3 tablespoons all-purpose flour	3 eggs, separated
1/2 teaspoon salt	1 cup shredded Swiss cheese
1/2 teaspoon dried leaf basil	1 (9-oz.) pkg. frozen cut green beans,
1/8 teaspoon pepper	cooked, drained

Preheat oven to 350°F (175°C). Butter a 2-quart soufflé dish or casserole or 6 individual soufflé dishes. In a medium heavy saucepan, melt 3 tablespoons butter or margarine. Sauté onion in saucepan until onion is tender but not browned. Stir in flour until blended. Add salt, basil and pepper. Mix well. Gradually stir in chicken broth and milk. Stir over medium heat until mixture is thickened and bubbly. Remove from heat. In a small bowl, slightly beat egg yolks. Gradually add about 1/2 cup thickened sauce to beaten egg yolks, stirring constantly. Stir egg yolk mixture into remaining thickened sauce in saucepan. Add cheese. Stir over low heat until cheese melts. Coarsely chop cooked green beans. Stir beans into cheese sauce. In a small bowl, beat egg whites until stiff but not dry. Stir a large spoonful of egg whites into bean mixture. Gently fold remaining whites into bean mixture. Pour into prepared soufflé dish. Bake 1 hour for a 2-quart soufflé or 35 to 40 minutes for individual soufflés, until a cake tester inserted off-center comes out clean. The top of the soufflé should be dry and crusty. Serve immediately. Makes 4 to 6 servings.

Honey-Lemon Beans

Unusually delicious sweet-and-sour beans to serve with roasts.

2 tablespoons butter or margarine
1 tablespoon water
2 tablespoons honey
1/2 teaspoon salt
1/4 teaspoon paprika
1/2 teaspoon grated lemon peel

1 apple, cored, diced
2/3 cup chopped onion
1 teaspoon cornstarch
1 tablespoon cold water
1 (16-oz.) can cut green beans, drained

In a medium saucepan, combine butter or margarine, water, honey, salt, paprika and lemon peel. Bring to a boil; reduce heat. Cover and simmer 10 minutes. Stir in apple and onion. Cover and simmer until apple is tender, about 10 minutes. In a small bowl, dissolve cornstarch in cold water. Gradually stir cornstarch mixture into apple mixture over low heat. Continue stirring until sauce thickens. Add green beans. Cover and simmer 5 minutes, stirring occasionally. Makes 3 or 4 servings.

How To Make Cheese Soufflé

1/To prevent egg yolks from curdling, stir a small amount of thickened sauce into beaten yolks before stirring yolks into the sauce.

2/After adding cheese and green beans to the sauce, fold in a large spoonful of beaten egg whites. Gently fold in remaining beaten egg whites until no large lumps remain.

Stringy Beans

Swiss cheese makes green beans as much fun to eat as cheese fondue.

1 lb. fresh green beans or
   2 (9-oz.) pkgs. frozen cut green beans
1/2 cup water
1/2 teaspoon salt
2 tablespoons butter or margarine
1 tablespoon finely chopped onion

1 tablespoon all-purpose flour
1 teaspoon salt
1/8 teaspoon white pepper
1 cup dairy sour cream
1 cup shredded Swiss cheese

Wash and break ends from fresh beans. Cut fresh beans into 1-inch pieces. Bring water and salt to a boil in a medium saucepan. Add beans; reduce heat. Cover and simmer until just tender, 10 to 15 minutes for fresh beans; 8 to 10 minutes for frozen beans. Drain well. Preheat oven to 350°F (175°C). In a medium saucepan, melt butter or margarine. Sauté onion in saucepan until tender but not browned. Stir in flour, salt and pepper. Add sour cream. Stir constantly over low heat until sauce thickens; do not boil. Fold in drained cooked beans. Turn into a 2-quart casserole with a cover. Bake in preheated oven 15 minutes. Remove cover, sprinkle with shredded cheese and bake uncovered 5 minutes. Makes 4 to 6 servings.

Zesty Green Beans

Enjoy these with hamburgers or fried chicken.

1 lb. fresh green beans or
   2 (9-oz.) pkgs. frozen green beans
1/2 cup water
1/2 teaspoon salt
3 slices bacon
2 tablespoons chopped canned pimiento
1 tablespoon pickle relish
2 teaspoons cornstarch

1 teaspoon sugar
1/4 teaspoon dry mustard
2 tablespoons red wine vinegar
1 teaspoon soy sauce
1 teaspoon Worcestershire sauce
2 drops Tabasco sauce
1/4 cup water

Break ends off fresh beans. Wash beans. In a large saucepan or skillet, bring 1/2 cup water with salt to a boil. Add beans. Cook until tender, about 15 minutes for fresh beans; about 10 minutes for frozen beans. Drain well. In a small skillet, fry bacon until crisp. Drain on paper towels. Pour off all but 2 tablespoons bacon drippings. Stir in pimiento and pickle relish. In a small bowl or measuring cup, combine cornstarch, sugar and dry mustard. Stir in vinegar, soy sauce, Worcestershire sauce, Tabasco sauce and water. Stir until smooth. Add cornstarch mixture to bacon drippings in skillet. Cook and stir until sauce is thickened and clear. Pour over beans. Heat thoroughly, about 5 minutes. Makes 4 to 6 servings.

Cauliflower Custard Bake

Bon Appètit, a seasoning blend, is sold with the spices and herbs in your supermarket.

1 fresh medium cauliflower	2 egg yolks
1 qt. cold water	1/4 cup dairy sour cream
1 tablespoon salt	3/4 cup milk
3-1/2 cups water	2 tablespoons butter or margarine, melted
1 teaspoon salt	1/2 teaspoon salt
1 (9-oz.) pkg. frozen cut green beans or	2 tablespoons diced pimiento
1 (10-oz.) pkg. frozen baby lima beans	1/4 teaspoon Bon Appètit seasoning

Remove leaves and stalk from cauliflower. Soak cauliflower in cold water with 1 tablespoon salt 10 minutes. In a medium saucepan, combine 1/2 cup water and 1/2 teaspoon salt. Bring to a boil. Add green beans or lima beans. Cook uncovered until crisp-tender, about 10 minutes; drain. In a large saucepan, combine 3 cups water and 1/2 teaspoon salt. Bring to a boil. Add cauliflower. Cook uncovered until tender, about 15 minutes; drain. Put green beans or lima beans in a 2-quart casserole. Separate cooked cauliflower into flowerets. Toss flowerets with cooked beans. In a small bowl, combine egg yolks, sour cream, milk, butter or margarine, salt, pimiento and Bon Appètit seasoning. Stir until smooth. Pour sour cream sauce over beans and cauliflower. Toss gently. Bake uncovered 20 minutes. Makes 4 to 6 servings.

Succotash

Indians taught early American settlers to combine beans and corn.

1 (10-oz.) pkg. frozen baby lima beans	1/4 teaspoon salt
1 (10-oz.) pkg. frozen whole-kernel corn	Pepper to taste
1 cup water	1 tablespoon all-purpose flour
1 teaspoon salt	1/2 cup chicken broth, warmed
2 tablespoons butter or margarine	1/2 cup milk or light cream

In 2 separate saucepans, combine 1/2 cup water and 1/2 teaspoon salt. Bring to a boil. Cook baby lima beans and corn separately in boiling salted water 10 minutes. Drain and combine in a 2-quart casserole; set aside. Preheat oven to 350°F (175°C). In a small saucepan, melt butter or margarine. Stir in 1/4 teaspoon salt, pepper and flour until smooth. Gradually add chicken broth, stirring constantly. Stir in milk or cream. Stir constantly over medium heat until mixture thickens and comes to a boil. Pour sauce over beans and corn. Bake 30 minutes. Makes 4 to 6 servings.

Eggplant Rolls

When eggplant slices are cooked, they become soft and will roll up easily.

2 cups drained, cooked garbanzo beans, page 15, or 1 (15-oz.) can garbanzo beans, drained
1 large eggplant
1/4 cup vegetable oil
1 cup cottage cheese
1 egg

1/2 cup cooked chopped fresh or frozen spinach, well-drained
1 tablespoon chopped fresh parsley
1/4 cup chopped green onions
1 teaspoon salt
1 cup Marinara Sauce, page 72
4 oz. mozzarella cheese, shredded

Prepare garbanzo beans. Cut off top of eggplant. Cut thin lengthwise slices from opposite sides of eggplant. Save these slices for another use. Peel remaining eggplant and cut lengthwise into 8 thin slices. Heat 1 tablespoon oil in a large skillet. Brush both sides of eggplant slices with oil. Cook about 3 minutes on each side until tender and softened, adding oil to skillet as needed. Preheat oven to 350°F (175°C). In a medium bowl, combine garbanzo beans, cottage cheese, egg, spinach, parsley, green onions and salt. Mix well. Spread about 1/4 cup bean mixture on each eggplant slice. Roll up from narrow end. Secure with wooden picks if necessary. Arrange rolls in a shallow baking dish. Prepare Marinara Sauce. Pour over eggplant rolls. Sprinkle cheese on top. Bake 30 minutes. Makes 4 to 8 servings.

Sprout & Bean Bake

Sprout your own mung beans or lentils, pages 12 and 13.

1/2 cup water
1/4 teaspoon salt
1 (9-oz.) pkg. frozen French-style green beans
2 cups mung bean sprouts or lentil sprouts
2 tablespoons vegetable oil
2 green onions, sliced

1/8 teaspoon garlic salt
1 (10-1/2-oz.) can cream of celery soup
1/2 cup water
2 cups fresh fine breadcrumbs, page 102
2 tablespoons butter or margarine
1/4 cup chopped cashew nuts

In a medium saucepan, bring 1/2 cup water and salt to a boil. Add beans. Cook 2 minutes. Drain and set aside. Rinse sprouts. Heat oil in a medium skillet. Add green onions and sprouts. Sprinkle with garlic salt. Stir over medium heat 3 minutes. Add cooked green beans; toss. In a small bowl, combine soup and 1/2 cup water. Pour over green bean mixture; toss again. Turn into a 2-quart casserole. Preheat oven to 400°F (205°C). In a medium skillet, toss breadcrumbs in butter or margarine until golden brown. Stir in cashew nuts. Sprinkle breadcrumb mixture over beans. Bake uncovered 30 minutes. Makes 4 servings.

How To Make Eggplant Rolls

1/With a long knife, cut off top of eggplant. Then cut a thin slice from 2 opposite sides of eggplant. Peel remaining eggplant with a paring knife. Cut lengthwise into thin slices.

2/Brush eggplant slices with oil before sautéing in a large skillet. Cook about 3 minutes on each side, adding oil as needed to prevent sticking or burning. Remove softened eggplant slices from skillet.

3/Spread about 1/4 cup garbanzo bean filling on each eggplant slice. Roll up, using both hands. Secure with a wooden pick if necessary.

International Dishes

Each culture has contributed special culinary skills and ingredients to bean cookery. Hummus, from the Middle East, wouldn't be authentic without sesame seeds. Garbanzo beans, cumin and red pepper are needed to make spicy South American Puchero. And the variety of fresh vegetables, olive oil and herbs add special flavor to Minestrone.

Recipes in this section are not necessarily authtic; they are representative. Some exotic ingredients are not readily available in all areas. In most cases, these have been replaced by more commonly available foods. We have also changed some cooking techniques to make preparation easier and less time-consuming.

In many countries, beans are a daily staple and a challenge to imaginative cooks. Garbanzo beans, also known as *chick peas* and *ceci beans*, were first used in Mediterranean countries. We enjoy their marvelous texture in Hummus and Antipasto Platter.

China can boast development of the mighty soybean because its uses and various products spread from China to neighboring countries and across oceans to other continents.

Mung bean sprouts are served in Oriental dishes all over the world. We have included the Chinese recipe for Egg Foo Yung so you can enjoy the marvelous flavor and texture that mung bean sprouts contribute.

Lentils probably have the longest history and widest distribution of all the legumes—from Egypt, across Europe and throughout the United States. They are still a strong influence in Middle Eastern and East European cooking. Try them in Black Forest Soup.

Hearty German Fare
Beer-Steamed Bratwurst
Spicy Brown Mustard
Caraway Rye Bread
Hot German Bean Salad, page 145
Sauerkraut Marinade, page 59
Lemon Ice Box Cake

Provincial French Dinner
Fresh Artichokes
With
Whipped Lemon Butter
Cassoulet, page 140
Tossed Vegetable Salad
With
Mustard French Dressing, page 69
Crusty French Rolls
Blueberry Cheesecake

Hummus

Serve this Middle Eastern spread with wedges of warm pita bread or cold cucumber rounds.

2 cups drained cooked garbanzo beans,
   page 15, or 1 (15-oz.) can garbanzo
   beans, drained
2 tablespoons lemon juice
1/2 teaspoon salt
1 tablespoon vegetable oil

1/3 cup cottage cheese
1/4 cup finely chopped onion
1 garlic clove, minced
1/4 cup chopped fresh parsley
1 tablespoon vegetable oil
2 tablespoons sesame seeds

Combine garbanzo beans, lemon juice, salt, 1 tablespoon oil and cottage cheese in blender. Blend until smooth. In a small skillet, sauté onion, garlic and parsley in 1 tablespoon oil until onion is tender but not browned. Stir into bean mixture. In a heavy skillet, toast sesame seeds over medium heat until golden, 3 to 5 minutes; see page 73. Watch carefully because the seeds burn quickly! Add toasted sesame seeds to bean mixture; stir. Serve at room temperature or chilled. Store leftover hummus in refrigerator. Makes about 2 cups.

Minestrone

Olive oil adds flavor and prevents the butter or margarine from burning.

1 lb. dried Great Northern beans
Water for soaking
2 (10-3/4-oz.) cans chicken broth
6 cups water
1 teaspoon salt
2 tablespoons olive oil
2 tablespoons butter or margarine
1 medium onion, cut in half lengthwise, sliced
2 garlic cloves, minced
2 carrots, cut in 1/4-inch slices
1 celery rib, sliced
1 leek, sliced, if desired

1 (16-oz.) can Italian plum tomatoes,
   undrained
1 tablespoon chopped fresh parsley
2 teaspoons dried leaf basil
1/2 teaspoon dried leaf oregano
1 teaspoon salt
1 medium zucchini, cut in 1/4-inch slices
1 fresh medium tomato, peeled, diced
1-1/2 cups shredded cabbage
1/2 cup uncooked elbow macaroni
Freshly grated Parmesan cheese

Sort and soak beans; see How To Prepare Dried Beans, pages 5 and 6. Drain beans; discard soak water. In a 4-quart pot, combine soaked beans, chicken broth, 6 cups water and 1 teaspoon salt. Bring to a boil; reduce heat. Cover and simmer until beans are tender, 1 to 1-1/2 hours. In a large skillet, combine olive oil and butter or margarine, heating slightly. Sauté onion, garlic, carrot, celery and leek, if desired, until onion is tender but not browned. Add Italian tomatoes, breaking them up with a fork. Stir in parsley, basil, oregano and 1 teaspoon salt. Cover and simmer 10 minutes. Add cooked vegetable mixture to beans. Cover and simmer 20 minutes. Add zucchini, fresh tomato, cabbage and macaroni. Stir well. Simmer uncovered 10 minutes. Sprinkle each serving with freshly grated Parmesan cheese. Makes 6 to 8 servings.

Pozole

Enjoy this Mexican stew as either a main dish or a first course.

1-1/2 cups dried pink beans or pinto beans
Water for soaking
1 slice bacon
1-1/2 to 2 lbs. beef neck bones
1 cup chopped onion
1 garlic clove, minced

3 cups water
4 beef bouillon cubes
1 teaspoon dried leaf oregano
1/4 cup chopped fresh cilantro or celery leaves
2 (15-oz.) cans white hominy, undrained
Salt to taste

Sort and soak beans; see How To Prepare Dried Beans, pages 5 and 6. Drain beans; discard soak water. In a large skillet, fry bacon until crisp. Drain on paper towels. Crumble bacon and set aside. Brown neck bones in bacon drippings. Remove and set aside. Sauté onion and garlic in skillet until onion is softened. In a 4-quart pot, combine soaked beans, crumbled bacon, browned neck bones, sautéed onion mixture, 3 cups water, bouillon cubes, oregano and cilantro or celery leaves. Bring to a boil; reduce heat. Cover and simmer 1-1/2 hours. Remove bones. Cut meat from bones and discard bones. Dice meat. Stir diced meat and hominy into stew. Simmer 1 hour longer. Add salt to taste. Makes 6 to 8 servings.

Pease Soup

The meat balls in this old English soup recipe are also used in Spicy Dip, page 22.

1 lb. green split peas
8 cups water
4 beef bouillon cubes
1 cup chopped onion
1 teaspoon salt
1/2 teaspoon dried leaf basil

1/2 teaspoon dried leaf marjoram
1/8 teaspoon pepper
5 celery leaves
Yeoman's Meatballs, see below
3 cups coarsely chopped fresh spinach

Yeoman's Meatballs:
1 lb. ground beef
1 egg
1 cup fresh fine breadcrumbs, page 102

1 teaspoon salt
1/2 teaspoon dried leaf basil

Sort and rinse peas. In a 4-quart pot, combine rinsed peas, water, bouillon cubes, onion, salt, basil, marjoram, pepper and celery leaves. Bring to a boil; reduce heat. Cover and simmer until peas are tender, about 45 minutes. Puree 2 cups of soup in blender or food processor. Return pureed soup to pot. Prepare meatballs and add to soup. Add chopped spinach; stir. Heat 15 minutes, stirring frequently. Makes 6 to 8 servings.

Yeoman's Meatballs:
Preheat oven to 350°F (175°C). In a medium bowl, combine beef, egg, breadcrumbs, salt and basil. Mix well. Shape into balls about the size of walnuts. Place on a rimmed baking sheet. Bake 15 minutes. Makes about 24 meatballs.

Black Forest Soup

A hearty, old-country soup made with sausage and beer.

2 cups dried lentils
6-1/2 cups water
1/2 cup chopped onion
1 garlic clove, minced
1 cup parsnip chunks or turnip chunks
2 tablespoons vegetable oil

1 (12-oz.) can beer
1/2 teaspoon dried leaf marjoram
1 teaspoon salt
1/2 lb. knackwurst or Polish sausage,
   cut in 1-inch slices

Sort and rinse lentils. In a 4-quart pot, combine rinsed lentils and water. In a medium skillet, sauté onion, garlic and parsnips or turnips in oil until onion is tender but not browned. Add sautéed onion mixture to lentils. Stir in beer, marjoram, salt and sausage slices. Bring to a boil; reduce heat. Cover and simmer until lentils are tender, about 45 minutes. Serve soup in heavy mugs or bowls. Makes 6 to 8 servings.

How To Make Pease Soup

1/Roll a rounded teaspoonful of meatball mixture into a ball. Place meatballs on a rimmed baking sheet or pizza pan so the drippings won't overflow into your oven.

2/Meatballs will bake to a deep brown in 15 minutes. Remove from baking sheet with a slotted spoon. Add cooked meatballs to Pease Soup.

Antipasto Platter

This Italian appetizer could be a meal in itself.

1 cup drained, cooked garbanzo beans,
  page 15, or 1 cup canned garbanzo
  beans, drained
1 cup drained, cooked Great Northern beans,
  page 15, or 1 cup canned cannellini
  beans, drained
4 cups Italian Marinade, see below
2 small onions, cut in quarters
1 small cauliflower, separated into flowerets
3 carrots, cut in 1/4-inch slices

1 green pepper, seeded,
  cut into 2" x 1/4" strips
1 large zucchini, cut in 1/4-inch slices
1 (4-oz.) can button mushrooms, drained
6 oz. salami, sliced
6 oz. Provolone cheese, sliced
12 to 16 black olives
Tuscan peppers or cherry peppers
1/3 cup Vinaigrette Dressing,
  page 70, if desired

Italian Marinade:
2 cups chicken broth
1 cup dry white wine
1/3 cup vegetable oil
2 tablespoons olive oil
1/2 cup vinegar

6 fresh parsley sprigs
2 garlic cloves, minced
1 teaspoon dried leaf oregano
1 teaspoon salt
6 whole black peppercorns

Prepare beans and Italian Marinade. Combine marinade, onions, cauliflowerets and carrots in a medium saucepan. Bring to a boil; reduce heat. Cover and simmer 3 minutes. Add green pepper and zucchini; bring to a boil again. Drain vegetables, reserving marinade. Place vegetables in a medium bowl. Add mushrooms. Combine garbanzo beans and Great Northern beans in a small bowl. Pour marinade over both vegetables and beans to cover. Refrigerate at least 6 hours or overnight. To serve, drain beans and vegetables, reserving marinade for storing leftovers. Arrange salami and cheese slices alternately around edge of a large platter. Pile beans in center of platter. Arrange vegetables around beans. Garnish with black olives and peppers. If desired, drizzle Vinaigrette Dressing over all. Makes 4 to 6 servings.

Italian Marinade:

In a 4-quart pot, combine all ingredients. Bring to a boil; reduce heat. Cover and simmer 10 minutes. Makes 4 cups.

Antipasto Mold

If the gelatin mixture is not thick enough, the vegetables and tuna will sink to the bottom.

2 cups drained cooked Great Northern beans,
    page 15, or 1 (15-oz.) can cannellini
    beans, drained
2 envelopes unflavored gelatin
1/4 cup cold water
3 cups chicken broth
1/4 cup vinegar

1/4 teaspoon garlic powder
1/2 teaspoon black pepper
1/2 cup sliced black olives
1/2 cup chopped green pepper
1 (6-1/2-oz.) can tuna, drained
1 small tomato, sliced
1 small onion, sliced, separated in rings

Prepare beans. In a medium bowl, dissolve gelatin in cold water. Add chicken broth and vinegar. Stir well. Stir in garlic powder and black pepper. Refrigerate gelatin until it thickens to the consistency of unbeaten egg whites. Stir in olives, green pepper, beans and tuna. Pour into a 6-cup mold and refrigerate until firm. To unmold, run a knife around edge of mold; place bottom of mold in warm water 5 seconds. Place a platter upside-down over mold. Invert platter and mold. Remove mold. Garnish with tomato slices and onion rings. Makes 8 servings.

Parisian Potato Salad

Use your prettiest glass serving bowl so the colorful layers can be seen.

4 medium red potatoes
1-1/2 cups water
1 teaspoon salt
1/2 to 3/4 cup Vinaigrette Dressing, page 70
1/2 cup water
1/2 teaspoon salt

3/4 lb. fresh green beans, cut in 1-inch pieces,
    or 1 (16-oz.) can cut green beans
1 cup slivered ham or roast beef
1/4 cup sliced green onion
3 radishes, sliced

Wash potatoes; do not peel. In a large saucepan, bring 1-1/2 cups water and 1 teaspoon salt to a boil. Add potatoes. Reduce heat. Cover and simmer 35 to 45 minutes until potatoes are tender. Prepare Vinaigrette Dressing. Remove potatoes from water with a slotted spoon. Cool slightly. Peel and slice. If using fresh green beans, bring 1/2 cup water and 1/2 teaspoon salt to a boil in a medium saucepan. Add fresh beans. Reduce heat. Cover and simmer 15 to 20 minutes until crisp-tender; drain. If using canned beans, drain; do not cook. In a glass serving bowl, alternate layers of cooked potato slices, cooked or canned green beans and ham or roast beef. Sprinkle each layer with green onion and radish slices. Drizzle with Vinaigrette Dressing. Refrigerate at least 4 hours or overnight. Makes 4 servings.

To substitute dried herbs for fresh herbs, use half as much of the dry herb.

Cassoulet

This French classic is the gourmet dish of beans.

1 lb. dried Great Northern beans
Water for soaking
2 (10-3/4-oz.) cans chicken broth
2-1/2 cups water
4 slices bacon, diced
2 garlic cloves, minced
2 whole cloves
2 medium onions, peeled, cut in quarters
2 medium carrots, peeled
1/2 teaspoon dried leaf thyme
2 large bay leaves

2 tablespoons chopped fresh parsley
2 tablespoons chopped celery leaves
2 teaspoons salt
1/8 teaspoon pepper
1 lb. Polish sausage
4 smoked pork chops or 1-1/2 lbs. ham,
    cut in 8 pieces
1 lb. bratwurst or knackwurst,
    cut in 2-inch pieces
1/2 cup dry white wine or
    additional chicken broth

Sort and soak beans; see How To Prepare Dried Beans, pages 5 and 6. Drain beans; discard soak water. In a 4-quart pot, combine soaked beans, 2 cans chicken broth and 2-1/2 cups water. In a medium skillet, fry bacon until crisp. Add cooked bacon and garlic to beans, reserving drippings. Stick cloves in onion pieces and add to beans. Cut each carrot in 2-inch pieces. Then cut each piece in half lengthwise. Add to beans. Make a bouquet garni by placing thyme, bay leaves, parsley and celery leaves in a 3-inch square of cheesecloth. Pull up corners of cheesecloth, twist together and tie with kitchen twine. Add bouquet garni, salt and pepper to beans. Bring to a boil; reduce heat. Cover and simmer until beans are tender, 1 to 1-1/2 hours. Remove onions, carrots and bouquet garni. Reserve onions and carrots to return to beans, if desired; discard cloves and bouquet garni. Drain beans, reserving liquid. Remove 1 cup beans and mash with a fork. Stir back into beans. With a sharp knife, make diagonal slashes about 1/8 inch deep in Polish sausage. In a medium skillet, brown pork chops or ham pieces and sausages in 1 tablespoon reserved bacon drippings. Preheat oven to 350°F (175°C). In a 3-quart casserole with a cover, put beans and onion and carrot, if desired. Stir in pieces of browned bratwurst or knackwurst. Sink brown chops or ham pieces into beans and around edges of casserole. Place browned Polish sausage on top of beans. Pour wine or chicken broth and reserved cooking liquid over cassoulet. Add water if necessary to almost cover beans. Bake 1 hour. Serve on deep rimmed plates or large shallow soup bowls. Cut polish sausage into serving pieces. For each serving, place a piece of pork or ham in a plate or bowl. Ladle beans next to pork. Top with a piece of sausage. Makes 8 servings.

If you have to leave the house unexpectedly while cooking beans, transfer them to a preheated slow cooker, set on Low. Finish cooking the beans on top of the stove when you return.

Egg Foo Yung

Making your own Chinese specialty isn't as difficult as you think.

3/4 cup fresh mung bean sprouts
Foo Yung Sauce, see below
4 eggs
4 fresh mushrooms, cut in 1/4-inch pieces

6 water chestnuts, diced
2 green onions, sliced
1/2 teaspoon salt
3 tablespoons vegetable oil

Foo Yung Sauce:
1 tablespoon cornstarch
2 tablespoons water
1 (10-3/4-oz.) can chicken broth

1/2 teaspoon salt
1/8 teaspoon pepper
1 tablespoon soy sauce

Rinse bean sprouts in cold water in a colander. Prepare Foo Yung Sauce. Beat eggs in a medium bowl with a fork. Stir in rinsed bean sprouts, mushrooms, water chestnuts, green onions and salt. In a wok or large skillet, heat 1 tablespoon oil. Pour about 1/4 cup egg mixture into hot oil. Cook 1 minute until lightly browned. Turn and cook 1 minute longer. Remove from wok or skillet and keep warm. Repeat until all egg mixture has been cooked, adding oil as needed. Serve hot with Foo Yung Sauce. Makes 4 servings.

Foo Yung Sauce:
In a small bowl, dissolve cornstarch in 2 tablespoons water. In a small saucepan, combine broth, salt, pepper, soy sauce and cornstarch mixture. Bring to a boil, stirring constantly; keep warm.

African Peanut Soup

Shallow bowls will show off the pretty colors of this distinctive soup.

1/2 cup dried baby lima beans
1/2 cup dried pea beans or small white beans
Water for soaking
1 cup dried black-eyed peas
8 cups water
1 cup sliced carrots
1 cup sliced celery
1/2 cup chopped onion

1/3 cup chopped green pepper
3 tablespoons vegetable oil
1-1/2 teaspoons salt
Cayenne pepper to taste
1-1/2 teaspoons dried leaf basil
1/2 teaspoon ground coriander
1 cup salted cocktail peanuts

Sort and soak small lima beans and pea beans or small white beans; see How To Prepare Dried Beans, pages 5 and 6. Drain beans; discard soak water. Sort and rinse black-eyed peas. In a 4-quart pot, combine soaked beans, rinsed black-eyed peas and 8 cups water. In a medium skillet, sauté carrots, celery, onion and green pepper in oil until onion is tender but not browned. Add sautéed vegetables to bean mixture. Stir in salt, cayenne pepper, basil and coriander. Bring to a boil; reduce heat. Cover and simmer until beans are tender, 1 to 1-1/2 hours. Add peanuts. Simmer 10 minutes longer. Makes 6 to 8 servings.

Chalupa

This is just one of many versions of Mexican beans and tortillas.

2 cups dried pinto beans
Water for soaking
1 lb. boneless pork
1 tablespoon vegetable oil
2 garlic cloves, minced
1 tablespoon ground cumin
1 teaspoon dried leaf oregano
2 tablespoons chili powder
1 (4-oz.) can diced or chopped green chilies

2 teaspoons salt
5 cups water
6 corn tortillas
Oil for frying
2 cups shredded lettuce
1 large tomato, diced
1 cup shredded Cheddar cheese
1/2 cup sliced black olives
1/4 cup dairy sour cream

Sort and soak beans; see How To Prepare Dried Beans, pages 5 and 6. Drain beans; discard soak water. In a large skillet, brown pork in oil until no longer pink. In a 4-quart pot, combine soaked beans, browned pork, garlic, cumin, oregano, chili powder, green chilies, salt and 5 cups water. Bring to a boil; reduce heat. Cover and simmer until beans and pork are tender, 1-1/2 to 2 hours, checking several times. Add more water as needed to keep beans covered while cooking. Remove pork from beans. Puree 1 cup of beans in blender, adding liquid from pot if necessary. Shred pork and add shredded meat to pot. Stir bean puree into bean-pork mixture. Simmer 30 minutes longer. Cut each tortilla into 6 pieces. Pour oil 1/2 inch deep into a heavy skillet. Fry tortilla pieces in hot oil until crisp. Drain fried chips on paper towels. To serve, mound bean mixture in center of each plate. Surround with shredded lettuce and diced tomato. Sprinkle with cheese and black olive slices. Top with a dollop of sour cream. Arrange chips on each plate around bean mixture. Use chips as scoops to eat bean mixture. Makes 4 servings.

Pasta e Fagioli

Pasta & Bean Soup *is the English translation of this Italian favorite.*

2 cups dried Great Northern beans
Water for soaking
1 oz. salt pork, diced
6 cups water
1 medium onion, cut in quarters, sliced
2 garlic cloves, minced
2 tablespoons olive oil

1 (28-oz.) can tomatoes, undrained
1-1/2 teaspoons Italian herb seasoning
1-1/2 teaspoons salt
1/4 teaspoon pepper
1 cup elbow or shell macaroni
6 tablespoons freshly grated Parmesan cheese

Sort and soak beans; see How To Prepare Dried Beans, pages 5 and 6. Drain beans; discard soak water. In a 4-quart pot, combine soaked beans, salt pork and 6 cups water. In a medium skillet, sauté onion and garlic in olive oil until onion is tender but not browned. Add sautéed onion mixture to beans. Bring to a boil; reduce heat. Cover and simmer until beans are tender, 1 to 1-1/2 hours. Add tomatoes, breaking up with a fork. Stir in Italian seasoning, salt, pepper and macaroni. Simmer 10 minutes until macaroni is just tender. Sprinkle about 1 tablespoon grated cheese over each serving. Makes 4 to 6 servings.

Mexican Chili Relleno Bake

It's pronounced chee-lay ray-ayn-oh *and it means* stuffed pepper.

2 cups dried black beans
Water for soaking
5 cups water
1/2 cup chopped onion
2 tablespoons vegetable oil
2 teaspoons salt
1/2 teaspoon dried leaf oregano
4 fresh Anaheim green chilies or
   2 (4-oz.) cans whole green roasted chilies

4 oz. Monterey Jack cheese
4 eggs
2/3 cup milk
6 tablespoons all-purpose flour
3/4 teaspoon baking powder
1/2 teaspoon salt
1/2 cup shredded Cheddar cheese
2 cups Spicy Tomato Sauce, page 72

Sort and soak beans; see How To Prepare Dried Beans, pages 5 and 6. Drain beans; discard soak water. In a large saucepan, combine soaked beans, 5 cups water, onion, oil, 2 teaspoons salt and oregano. Bring to a boil; reduce heat. Cover and simmer until beans are tender, 1 to 1-1/2 hours. **To roast fresh chilies,** place under broiler until skin blisters. Cooling in a plastic bag will help loosen skins. Peel off charred skins with a sharp knife. Remove seeds and membranes from chilies. **If using canned chilies,** wash chilies, then remove membranes and seeds. Drain beans, reserving about 1 cup cooking liquid. In a medium bowl, coarsely mash beans with a potato masher, adding 1/2 to 1 cup reserved cooking liquid for desired consistency. Spread mashed beans in the bottom of a 2-quart casserole. Preheat oven to 375°F (190°C). Cut Monterey Jack cheese into 4 strips and stuff into prepared chilies. Place stuffed chilies on top of beans. In a medium bowl, beat eggs with electric mixer on medium speed until foamy. Add milk. Beat to combine. Add flour, baking powder and 1/2 teaspoon salt. Beat until smooth. Pour egg mixture over chilies. Sprinkle with Cheddar cheese. Bake 40 minutes. Prepare Spicy Tomato Sauce. Serve sauce separately to pour over each serving as desired. Makes 4 to 6 servings.

Italian Tuna Salad

A tasty budget stretcher for tuna fish.

4 cups drained cooked pea beans or
   small white beans, page 15, or
   2 (15-oz.) cans cannellini beans, drained
1/4 to 1/3 cup Italian Salad Dressing,
   page 66
3 green onions, finely chopped

2 tablespoons chopped fresh parsley
1/4 cup sliced pimiento-stuffed olives
1 (6-1/2-oz.) can tuna fish
Lettuce cups or other salad greens
1 (12-oz.) jar marinated vegetables, if desired

Prepare beans and Italian Salad Dressing. In a large bowl, combine beans, green onions, parsley and olives. Pour salad dressing over bean mixture. Toss gently to keep beans whole. Cover and refrigerate at least 6 hours or overnight. To serve, drain tuna and break into chunks. Add to bean mixture. Toss lightly. Arrange salad in lettuce cups or on salad greens. If desired, garnish with marinated vegetables. Makes 4 to 6 servings.

Hot German Bean Salad

Something special to go with spicy sausages or hot dogs.

4 cups Savory White Beans made with
   large lima beans, page 18
6 slices bacon
1/2 cup chopped onion
1/2 cup vinegar

1/2 cup chicken broth
1/8 teaspoon pepper
1 teaspoon sugar
1 egg yolk, slightly beaten

Prepare beans; drain. Put in a 1-1/2-quart casserole; keep warm. In a medium skillet, fry bacon until crisp. Drain on paper towels. Add onion to bacon drippings. Sauté until onion is tender but not browned. Stir in vinegar, chicken broth, pepper and sugar. Bring mixture to a boil. Stir in egg yolk. Pour over beans in casserole. Crumble bacon and sprinkle over beans; stir gently. Serve salad warm. Makes 4 to 6 servings.

How To Make
Mexican Chili Relleno Bake

1/Grasp and pull or cut membranes from peeled, roasted fresh green chilies or canned whole green chilies.

2/Push a strip of Monterey Jack cheese into each chili. Place stuffed chilies on top of mashed beans. Pour egg mixture over chilies. Sprinkle with cheese before baking.

Caldo Gallego

Cornmeal is the thickener for this hearty Spanish soup.

2 cups dried baby lima beans
Water for soaking
8 cups water
4 chicken bouillon cubes
1 meaty ham shank, cut in 3 or 4 pieces
1 chicken breast or leg including thigh
2 garlic cloves, minced

1/2 cup chopped onion
1 large tomato, peeled, cut in quarters
2 medium potatoes, peeled, cubed
2 cups shredded cabbage
1 tablespoon cornmeal
1/2 teaspoon salt

Sort and soak beans; see How To Prepare Dried Beans, pages 5 and 6. Drain beans; discard soak water. In a heavy 4-quart pot, combine 8 cups water and bouillon cubes. Bring to a boil and continue to boil until bouillon is dissolved. Add soaked beans, ham shank pieces and chicken. If using a chicken leg, separate thigh and drumstick. Stir in garlic and onion. Bring to a boil; reduce heat. Cover and simmer until beans are tender, 1 to 1-1/2 hours. Add tomato and potatoes. Simmer 30 minutes. Remove ham shank and chicken pieces. Cut meat from bones and discard bones. Dice meat. Add shredded cabbage and diced ham and chicken to soup. Simmer 10 minutes. Stir in cornmeal to thicken. Cook and stir 5 minutes. Season with salt. Makes 6 to 8 servings.

Puchero

Instead of flying to Argentina, enjoy this robust meal-in-a-bowl at your own table.

2 cups dried garbanzo beans
Water for soaking
2 tablespoons vegetable oil
1/2 lb. stewing beef, cut in 1/2-inch cubes
1/2 lb. pork, cut in 1/2-inch cubes
1/2 cup chopped onion
2 garlic cloves, minced
8 cups water
4 chicken bouillon cubes

1/4 teaspoon cumin seeds or ground cumin
1 dried red pepper or
    1/8 teaspoon cayenne pepper
1 medium potato, peeled, cubed
1 medium tomato, peeled, diced
1 small green pepper, seeded, sliced
1 (10-oz.) pkg. frozen whole-kernel corn
1 teaspoon salt

Sort and soak beans; see How To Prepare Dried Beans, pages 5 and 6. Drain beans; discard soak water. In a large skillet, heat vegetable oil. Brown beef and pork cubes until no longer pink. Remove meat and set aside. Sauté onion and garlic in drippings until onion is softened. In a 4-quart pot, combine soaked beans, browned meat, sautéed onion mixture, 8 cups water, bouillon cubes, cumin and red pepper or cayenne pepper. Bring to a boil; reduce heat. Cover and simmer until beans and meat are tender, 1 to 1-1/2 hours. Add potato, tomato, green pepper, corn and salt. Simmer 30 minutes longer before serving. Makes 4 to 6 servings.

Variation

Use 2 (15-ounce) cans garbanzo beans in place of 2 cups dried garbanzo beans. Do not soak or cook canned beans. Drain beans. Cook meat with bouillon mixture until tender, then add beans with vegetables. Simmer 30 minutes before serving.

Pedro's Special

Top these Mexican treats with taco sauce or Green Chili Salsa, page 69.

2 cups Refried Beans, page 18, or
   1 (17-oz.) can refried beans
1 lb. lean ground beef
1 teaspoon chili powder
1/2 teaspoon ground cumin
1 teaspoon salt
1 teaspoon all-purpose flour

1/3 cup beef broth or tomato sauce
8 taco shells
4 cups shredded lettuce
2 fresh medium tomatoes, diced
1 cup shredded Longhorn cheese
1 cup taco sauce

Prepare Refried Beans and keep warm. In a large skillet, brown ground beef until no longer pink. Spoon off any excess fat. In a small bowl, combine chili powder, cumin, salt and flour. Sprinkle flour mixture over browned beef and stir to coat. Stir in broth or tomato sauce. Cover and simmer 10 minutes, stirring occasionally. To make tacos, hold taco shells in one hand. Fill with about 1/4 cup warm beans, 1/4 cup beef mixture, 1 large spoonful lettuce, 1 spoonful tomatoes and a sprinkle of cheese. Drizzle with taco sauce. Makes 8 tacos.

Variations

Pedro's Tostadas: Fry 6 corn tortillas in oil in a skillet until crisp. Drain on paper towels. Place a crisp tortilla on a plate. Spread with about 1/3 cup warm beans. Sprinkle with about 1/3 cup beef mixture. Mound lettuce on top of beef. Sprinkle diced tomato and cheese on lettuce. Drizzle with taco sauce. Makes 6 tostadas.

Pedro's Burritos: Preheat oven to 350°F (175°C). Wrap six 10-inch flour tortillas in foil. Heat in oven 15 minutes. Place 1 tortilla on a flat surface. Spread about 1/3 cup beans on tortilla near one edge. Cover with about 1/3 cup beef mixture. Top with tomato and a sprinkle of cheese. Fold edge nearest filling over until filling is just covered. Fold over 2 sides envelope-fashion and roll up. Place burritos on a baking sheet. Bake until heated through, about 15 minutes. To serve, mound shredded lettuce on each plate. Place a warm burrito on each lettuce mound. Top with a spoonful of taco sauce. Makes 6 burritos.

Breads & Desserts

Pureed beans added to home-baked bread improve its flavor, texture and nutritional content. The puree also gives a moistness and tenderness you would not have thought possible. Whole-grain breads, which tend to be heavy with a coarse texture, are greatly improved by adding pureed beans. Pinto Wheat Bread is a delicious whole-wheat bread that will stay fresh and moist for as long as 4 or 5 days. In addition to Bean Puree, Colonial Bread contains cornmeal, rye and whole-wheat flour. It has become a favorite at our house.

Beans make quickbreads, such as cornbread or biscuits, unusual treats. Serve Bean Fritters to add pizzazz to Sunday's roast beef and mashed potatoes. BBQ Biscuits with grilled pork chops will delight guests at your next barbecue.

At first thought, beans and desserts seem incompatible. Not so! What beans do for breads, they can also do for pies and cakes. Desserts made with Bean Puree are scrumptiously moist. Spices and sweeteners such as brown sugar modify the bean taste enough so you're not aware of beans. You would never suspect that beans were used to make Apple Surprise Cake, Spicy Zucchini Bread and Brown Sugar Pie. The next time you have a family get-together for a special occasion, add one of the desserts from this section to your menu. You'll be amazed at the compliments!

Dinner With Friends
Cheddar-Stuffed Meatloaf
Scalloped Potatoes
Confetti Beans, page 126
Brown Sugar Pie, page 157

Wayfarer's Welcome
Pioneer Stew, page 94
Fresh Orange & Pineapple Salad
on Lettuce
Bean Fritters, page 153
Caramel Baked Custard

Pinto Wheat Bread

Make this in a loaf pan or shape it into a round loaf. Or double the recipe and make one of each.

1 cup Bean Puree made with pinto beans,
  page 18
1 cup lukewarm water
1 tablespoon honey
1 pkg. active dry yeast

2 tablespoons vegetable oil
1 teaspoon salt
2 cups whole-wheat flour
3/4 to 1-1/2 cups all-purpose flour

Prepare Bean Puree. In a large bowl, combine water and honey, stirring to mix completely. Dissolve yeast in honey-water mixture. Let stand until foamy. Stir in Bean Puree, vegetable oil and salt. Add whole-wheat flour. Mix well. Stir in all-purpose flour until dough is stiff. Turn out onto a lightly floured surface and knead until smooth and elastic. Return dough to bowl. Lightly butter top of dough and let rise until doubled in bulk. Grease a 9" x 5" loaf pan or baking sheet. Punch down dough and knead 3 to 4 times until easy to handle. Shape into a loaf. Place in loaf pan or on baking sheet. Cover and let rise until doubled in bulk, about 45 minutes. Preheat oven to 350°F (175°C). Bake bread until golden brown, about 50 minutes. Remove from pan or baking sheet. Cool on a rack. May be stored in an airtight plastic bag at room temperature or in the refrigerator. Makes 1 loaf.

How To Make Pinto Wheat Bread

1/When bread dough has risen about double its original bulk, press your fist into the risen dough to punch down. Remove punched down dough from the bowl.

2/After kneading on a lightly floured surface, shape dough into a smooth loaf by pulling the sides and edges under while pressing into the desired shape.

Dilled Bean Bread

Good served warm with butter and great for sandwiches!

1 cup Bean Puree made with Great Northern beans, page 18	1 cup lukewarm water 2 tablespoons sugar
2 tablespoons butter or margarine	3-1/2 to 4 cups all-purpose flour
2 tablespoons finely minced or grated onion	1 egg, slightly beaten
1 teaspoon salt	1/2 tablespoon coarse salt
2 teaspoons dried dill weed	2 tablespoons grated Parmesan cheese
1 pkg. active dry yeast	1 tablespoon chopped parsley

Prepare Bean Puree. Melt butter or margarine in a medium skillet. Sauté onion in skillet until tender but not browned. Stir in Bean Puree, salt and dill weed. Mix well. Remove from heat and cool to lukewarm. In a large bowl, dissolve yeast in lukewarm water. Stir in sugar. When bean mixture has cooled, add to yeast mixture. Stir in flour to make a stiff dough. Turn dough onto a lightly floured surface and knead until smooth and elastic. Return dough to bowl. Lightly butter top of dough and let rise until doubled in bulk. Grease a 9" x 5" loaf pan. Punch down dough and shape into a loaf. Place in greased loaf pan. With a sharp knife or single-edge razor blade, make several diagonal slashes about 1/4 inch deep in top of loaf. Brush top of loaf with beaten egg. Combine salt, cheese and parsley in a small bowl. Sprinkle over loaf. Cover and let rise until doubled in bulk, 30 to 45 minutes. Preheat oven to 375°F (190°C). Bake until loaf is golden brown and sounds hollow when tapped, 30 to 40 minutes. Remove from pan. Cool on a rack. May be stored in an airtight plastic bag at room temperature or in the refrigerator. Makes 1 loaf.

Colonial Bread

This loaf freezes well. Bring it to room temperature before warming or serving.

1 cup Bean Puree made with pinto beans, page 18	2 tablespoons vegetable oil 1 pkg. active dry yeast
1 cup water	1/4 cup lukewarm water
1/4 cup yellow cornmeal	1/2 cup whole-wheat flour
3 tablespoons sugar	1/2 cup rye flour
1-1/2 teaspoons salt	2 to 2-1/2 cups all-purpose flour

Prepare Bean Puree. Bring water to a boil in a small saucepan. Stir in cornmeal, sugar, salt, Bean Puree and oil. Let cool to lukewarm. Dissolve yeast in lukewarm water and let stand until foamy. In a large bowl, combine Bean Puree mixture and yeast mixture. Add whole-wheat flour and rye flour, mixing well. Stir in all-purpose flour until dough is stiff. Turn dough onto a lightly floured surface and knead until smooth and elastic. Return dough to bowl. Lightly butter top of dough. Cover and let rise until doubled in bulk. Grease a 9" x 5" loaf pan. Punch down dough and shape into a loaf. Place loaf in pan. Cover and let rise until doubled in bulk. Preheat oven to 375°F (190°C). Bake until loaf is golden brown and sounds hollow when tapped, about 45 minutes. Remove from pan. Cool on a rack. May be stored in an airtight plastic bag at room temperature or in the refrigerator. Makes 1 loaf.

BBQ Biscuits

Gentle kneading will make these biscuits light and tall.

1/2 cup drained, chopped cooked red kidney
   beans, page 15, or 1/2 cup drained,
   chopped canned red kidney beans
2 cups sifted all-purpose flour
3 teaspoons baking powder

1 teaspoon salt
1/3 cup shortening
1/4 cup chili sauce
3/4 cup milk
1 teaspoon Worcestershire sauce

Prepare red kidney beans. Preheat oven to 450°F (230°C). Sift together flour, baking powder and salt into a medium bowl. Cut in shortening with a pastry blender or 2 knives until dough resembles cornmeal. Stir in beans. Add chili sauce, milk and Worcestershire sauce. Stir until flour mixture is just moistened. Turn onto a lightly floured surface. Gently knead dough with fingertips 15 times. Roll out dough 1/2 inch thick. Cut with a round 2-inch biscuit cutter or cookie cutter. Place biscuits on an ungreased baking sheet. Bake 12 to 15 minutes until lightly browned. Serve warm. Makes about 12 biscuits.

Harvest Pie

Remember this recipe when you want to make pumpkin pie but you don't have any pumpkin!

2 cups Bean Puree made with pinto beans,
   page 18
3 eggs
1-1/4 cups whole milk
1 (5-1/3-oz.) can evaporated milk
1 cup sugar
1/2 teaspoon salt

1 teaspoon ground cinnamon
1 teaspoon ground ginger
1/4 teaspoon ground cloves
1/4 teaspoon ground nutmeg
1 (9-inch) unbaked pie shell
Whipped cream

Prepare Bean Puree. Preheat oven to 375°F (190°C). In a large bowl, beat eggs until frothy. Add Bean Puree, whole milk and evaporated milk. Stir until smooth. Add sugar, salt, cinnamon, ginger, cloves and nutmeg. Stir until blended. Pour into unbaked pie shell. Bake 1 hour or until knife inserted in center comes out clean. Cool to room temperature before refrigerating. Serve chilled with a dollop of whipped cream. Makes 1 pie.

If beans cooked in a pressure cooker overcook, use them to make Bean Puree, page 18.

Corned Beef Pasties

English workers wrap pasties, or meat pies, in newspaper to keep them warm and take them to work.

2 cups drained cooked black-eyed peas,
    page 15, or 1 (15-oz.) can black-eyed
    peas, drained
Flaky Pastry, see below
1/3 cup water
1/4 teaspoon salt
1 medium potato, peeled, diced

2 tablespoons chopped onion
1 tablespoon bacon drippings or vegetable oil
2 cups shredded cabbage
1 (8-oz.) can corned beef, diced or shredded
1/2 teaspoon salt
Pepper to taste
2 to 3 tablespoons milk

Flaky Pastry:
2 cups sifted all-purpose flour
1 teaspoon salt

2/3 cup shortening
1/3 to 1/2 cup cold water

Prepare black-eyed peas. Prepare Flaky Pastry; set aside. In a small saucepan, bring water and salt to a boil. Add potato. Cook until almost tender, about 15 minutes; drain. In a medium skillet, sauté onion in bacon drippings or oil until tender but not browned. Add cooked potato, cabbage, corned beef, black-eyed peas, salt and pepper. Stir gently. Cover and simmer 10 minutes. Preheat oven to 350°F (175°C). On a lightly floured surface, roll out half of the Flaky Pastry 1/16 to 1/8 inch thick. Using a small bowl or plate as a guide, cut 5 or 6 circles about 4 inches in diameter. Place about 1/4 cup corned beef mixture on the center of each circle. Fold circles in half over filling. Crimp and seal edges with a fork. Place on an ungreased baking sheet. Repeat with remaining pastry and filling. Brush tops of pasties with milk. Bake 20 to 30 minutes until golden brown. Serve warm. Makes 10 to 12 pasties.

Flaky Pastry:

In a medium bowl, combine flour and salt. Add half of the shortening. With a pastry blender or 2 knives, cut shortening into flour until mixture resembles cornmeal. Cut in remaining shortening until mixture resembles large peas. Sprinkle cold water 1 tablespoon at a time over mixture, tossing with a fork. Dough should be just moist enough to hold together when pressed with a fork. Shape into a ball.

Bean Fritters

Change your biscuit or dinner roll routine and try these vegetable fritters.

Oil for deep frying
1 cup sifted all-purpose flour
3/4 teaspoon salt
1 teaspoon baking powder
1 egg, separated

1/2 cup milk
1 tablespoon butter or margarine, melted
1 cup frozen cut green beans, thawed
1 cup chopped carrots

Heat oil for deep frying to 350°F (175°C). At this temperature, a 1-inch cube of bread will turn golden brown in 65 seconds. In a medium bowl, combine flour, salt and baking powder. In a small bowl, mix egg yolk, milk and melted butter or margarine. Add to flour mixture. Mix until flour mixture is just moistened. In a small bowl, beat egg white until stiff. Fold beaten egg white into batter. Gently stir in green beans and carrots. Drop batter by small spoonfuls into hot oil. Fry until golden brown. Drain on paper towels. Serve warm. Makes 16 to 20 small fritters.

How To Make Corned Beef Pasties

1/Roll out Flaky Pastry on a lightly floured surface. With a paring knife, trace around a custard cup, small bowl, saucer or a round cardboard pattern about 4 inches in diameter.

2/Place about 1/4 cup corned beef mixture in center of each pastry circle. Fold circles over filling. Seal edges with a fork. Place pasties on an ungreased baking sheet.

Apple Surprise Cake

You won't believe it until you try it!

1 cup Bean Puree made with pinto beans,
    page 18
1/2 cup shortening
1 cup sugar
1 egg
1/2 cup apple butter
1-1/2 cups sifted all-purpose flour
2 teaspoons baking powder
1/2 teaspoon salt

1 teaspoon ground cinnamon
1/2 teaspoon ground cloves
1/2 teaspoon ground allspice
1 cup diced, peeled apple
Coffee Icing, see below
2 tablespoons lemon juice
2 tablespoons water
1 apple, unpeeled, cored, sliced thin
Pecan or walnut halves

Coffee Icing:

4 cups powdered sugar
4 tablespoons butter or margarine

Pinch of salt
4 to 5 tablespoons strong coffee

Prepare Bean Puree. Grease three 8-inch, round cake pans. Preheat oven to 350°F (175°C). In a medium bowl, cream shortening and sugar until light and fluffy. Add egg; continue beating until light. Stir in Bean Puree and apple butter. Sift together flour, baking powder, salt, cinnamon, cloves and allspice into a medium bowl. Stir flour mixture into bean mixture until blended. Mix in diced apple. Pour into greased pans. Bake 30 to 40 minutes or until a wooden pick inserted in center comes out clean. Cool in pans 10 minutes. Remove cakes from pans. Cool on racks. Prepare Coffee Icing. Layer cakes with Coffee Icing in between and on top layer. In a small bowl, combine water and lemon juice. Dip apple slices into lemon juice mixture to prevent darkening. Arrange apple slices and nuts on top of cake. Makes one 3-layer cake.

Coffee Icing:

In a small bowl, combine powdered sugar, butter or margarine and salt. Beat with electric mixer on low speed until blended. Add 3 to 4 tablespoons coffee. Beat until smooth. Beat in remaining coffee 1 teaspoon at a time as needed for spreading consistency.

Variation

To make a sheet cake, bake in a greased 13" x 9" baking pan 40 to 50 minutes. Cool cake in pan. Prepare only half the icing. Cover top of cooled cake with icing. Makes 1 sheet cake.

Skillet Bread

One skillet acts as a sauté pan, a baking pan and a serving dish!

1 cup drained, cooked black beans, page 15	2/3 cup milk
1/2 cup chopped onion	1/3 cup shortening, melted
1 garlic clove, minced	3/4 cup cornmeal
1 tablespoon vegetable oil	1/2 teaspoon baking soda
2 eggs	1/2 teaspoon salt
1 cup cream-style corn	3/4 cup shredded Cheddar cheese

Prepare black beans. Preheat oven to 350°F (175°C). In a medium cast iron or other ovenproof skillet, sauté onion and garlic in oil until onion is tender but not browned. Add beans. Mix well; set aside. In a medium bowl, beat eggs until frothy. Stir in corn, milk and melted shortening. Add cornmeal, baking soda and salt. Stir until just blended. Pour into skillet. Add bean mixture and 1/2 cup cheese. Mix slightly. Spread batter evenly in skillet. Sprinkle with remaining cheese. Bake 15 minutes. Cut in wedges and serve hot from the skillet. Makes 6 servings.

Spicy Zucchini Bread

A tasty moist bread to go with a luncheon salad such as Turkey Toss, page 61.

1 cup Bean Puree made with pinto beans, page 18	1 teaspoon vanilla extract
3 eggs	2 cups sifted all-purpose flour
1-1/2 cups sugar	1 teaspoon salt
1 cup vegetable oil	1 teaspoon baking soda
1-1/2 cups shredded zucchini	2-1/2 teaspoons baking powder
	2 teaspoons ground cinnamon

Prepare Bean Puree. Grease two 9" x 5" loaf pans. Preheat oven to 350°F (175°C). In a large bowl, combine eggs, sugar and oil. Beat with an electric mixer until smooth. Add zucchini, Bean Puree and vanilla. Sift together flour, salt, baking soda, baking powder and cinnamon. Add to bean mixture. Stir until blended. Pour into greased pans. Bake 40 to 50 minutes or until a wooden pick inserted in center comes out clean. Remove from pan. Cool on a rack. May be stored in an airtight plastic bag at room temperature or in the refrigerator. Makes 2 loaves.

Variation

Spicy Carrot Bread: Substitute 1 cup shredded carrot for 1-1/2 cups shredded zucchini.

Brown Sugar Pie

If you don't tell them what's in it, they'll think it's ordinary Chess Pie.

1 cup Bean Puree made with pinto beans,
   page 18
1/2 cup butter or margarine
1 cup packed brown sugar
3 eggs, separated

1 teaspoon vanilla extract
1 (9-inch) unbaked pie shell
1/8 teaspoon cream of tartar
1/3 cup packed brown sugar
1 teaspoon vanilla extract

Prepare Bean Puree. Preheat oven to 350°F (175°C). In a medium bowl, cream butter or margarine and 1 cup brown sugar with electric mixer on medium speed until light and fluffy. Beat in egg yolks. Stir 1 teaspoon vanilla into Bean Puree. Add Bean Puree to brown sugar mixture. Pour into unbaked pie shell. Bake 45 to 60 minutes until a knife inserted in pie comes out clean. Set pie aside. Pie puffs during baking and may settle a little as it cools. In a medium bowl, beat egg whites with electric mixer on high speed until frothy. Add cream of tartar. Continue beating while gradually adding 1/3 cup brown sugar and 1 teaspoon vanilla. Beat until meringue peaks round over when beaters are removed. Drop meringue by spoonfuls over hot pie. Spread over top of pie, sealing to edges of crust. Bake 10 to 15 minutes until meringue is lightly browned. Cool away from drafts. Serve at room temperature. Refrigerate cooled pie. Makes 1 pie.

Index

Index